The Century in Food

America's Fads and Favorites

BEVERLY BUNDY

PORTLAND, OREGON

DEDICATION

For my parents, Dorothy Rayborn Bundy
and James Harold Bundy, who made the world my oyster.

ACKNOWLEDGMENTS

THIS BOOK ORIGINATED as a series I wrote for *The Fort Worth Star-Telegram* in 1999. Without the support of my editors, Catherine Newton and Julie Haeberlin, there would have been no series. And a special place in the editor Pantheon is certainly reserved for Cathy Frisinger who inherited me just as the going was getting very tough on this project.

Without the good humor, the organization and the reading of fine print by Catherine Gulley, who helps make the daylight hours of my life run reasonably close to schedule, the series would have never won awards.

Gaile Robinson, who is always there when I need to vent and who dispenses love pats and tough love in equally effective doses.

Charles Caple, who has the good sense to worry when both the Food Editor and the Home Editor are not in their assigned seats.

Renie Steves, who was so very patient at the beginning and who is one of my biggest cheerleaders (in the most ladylike way) today.

Dr. Emilio Bombay, for being the best friend a Luddite girl could have.

Brill Bundy, who let me write the first book.

Chris Wienandt, for wrangling life so that I could have a modicum of peace, quiet, and the occasional creative thought.

And lastly, James Joseph Bundy Wienandt, who will have this story to know where we have been.

Copyright © 2002 Collectors Press, Inc.

Library of Congress Cataloging-in-Publication Data

Bundy, Beverly.
  The century in food : America's fads and favorites / by Beverly Bundy.— 1st American ed.
     p. cm.
  Includes bibliographical references.
  ISBN 1-888054-67-0 (Hardcover : alk. paper)
  1. Gastronomy—History. 2. Food habits—United States—History. I. Title.
  TX633 .B86 2003
  394.1'0973—dc21

                              2002005731

Design: Trina Stahl
Editor: Sue Mann

Printed in China
First American edition
9 8 7 6 5 4 3 2 1

Collectors Press books are available at special discounts for bulk purchases, premiums, and promotions. Special editions, including personalized inserts or covers, and corporate logos, can be printed in quantity for special purposes. For further information contact:
Special Sales, Collectors Press, Inc., P.O. Box 230986, Portland, OR 97281.
Toll-free: 1-800-423-1848

For a free catalog write: Collectors Press, Inc., P.O. Box 230986, Portland, OR 97281.
Toll-free: 1-800-423-1848 or visit our website at: www.collectorspress.com

Contents

Introduction

THIS BOOK BEGAN as a newspaper series for *Fort Worth Star-Telegram*. It was intended to be a century-end look at the inventions, innovations, and ingenuity that fueled American appetites for the century. It turned out to be the best history class I ever attended.

In 1999, when this series was written, America had finally found its own, formidable culinary voice. Regional chefs had, since the 1980s, delved into their local pantries and discovered a plethora of ingredients. Fiddlehead ferns, stone-ground grits, and Big Jim chilies joined the pantheon of Tuscan olive oil and French foie gras. We could, by God, cook with the big dogs.

But that was hardly the whole story.

The nation was packed with fast-food restaurants—McDonald's, Pizza Hut, Taco Bell—an international cuisine of another sort. Our supermarkets were huge, averaging 35,000 to 50,000 square feet. An estimated 25,000 new food products were introduced to a hungry public every year. The public was so inundated with food that by the end of the century some studies showed that 50 percent of all Americans were overweight.

Yet Americans have the lowest food costs in the world, spending only 10 percent of their income on food.

At the beginning of the century most cooking was done in fireplaces or, at best, on wood- or coal-fueled ranges. If you didn't have a servant, you most likely were a servant. Our foremothers and -fathers worked to put food on the table.

There was hardly a lack of food. America has never suffered a famine as sweeping as the one that devastated Ireland. Our rivers and coasts were teeming with fish and other seafood. Visiting Europeans wrote of being stunned at the amount of meat Americans consumed. Our virgin farmlands were rich with nutrients.

In fact, at the beginning of the century there was enough food so that Americans were already beginning to examine the way they ate. John Harvey Kellogg's Michigan sanatorium was in full swing, removing meat from the diet and adding more grain. America had so much food that its citizens could make choices.

And what were the choices they made? Come along and see.

AMERICA STRODE INTO the 20th century proud of its industry, sure of its science, and cocky with its prosperity. It was a country with an appetite for everything.

One percent of the population controlled fifty percent of the nation's wealth. For that segment, America was a land of plenty, and the Diamond Jim Bradys of the world wanted more than their fair share.

For financier Brady, breakfast was eggs, breads, muffins, grits, pancakes, steaks, chops, fried potatoes, and a pitcher of orange juice. At his midmorning snack, he ate two or three dozen oysters. His restaurant lunch (often at New York City's Delmonico's) was more oysters, and clams, lobsters, crabs, a joint of meat, pie, and more orange juice.

Dinner was the main event, however, when he'd again eat three dozen oysters, a dozen crabs, six or seven lobsters, terrapin soup, a steak, coffee, a tray of pastries, and two pounds of candy. (When Brady died at age fifty-six, his stomach was said to be six times larger than the average man's. Fittingly, he left the bulk of his estate to Johns Hopkins University.)

Brady was often accompanied by his longtime friend Lillian Russell, a popular stage actress who was the era's epitome of female beauty. Russell was known to match Brady forkful for forkful. The fair Lillian also smoked 500 cigars a month.

This couple was not alone in their conspicuous display of caloric consumption. The New York Riding Club hosted a "horse dinner" in the fourth-floor ballroom of Louis Sherry's restaurant. Horses were brought to the room in freight elevators, hitched to a large dining table, and fed oats while their riders ate fourteen-course dinners and sipped champagne out of bottles stashed in the saddlebags.

But not for the first time in Americans' table matters, and certainly not for the last, was there another segment of the population eating a very different diet. William and John Kellogg had introduced cornflakes by the  end of the previous century and were promoting the cereal at their sanatorium at Battle Creek, Mich. (Searching for the fountain of youth through diets was not a brainchild of the 21st century. Americans have, throughout their industrialized history, grasped at longevity and health through food fads.) Later, a former patient of the sanatorium, C. W. Post, introduced his take on the benefits of cereal by producing a caffeine-free beverage made from cereal he called Postum and by producing Grape-Nuts. All these products were promoted as being healthful.

Ah—manna from heaven—these breakfast foods didn't need to be

ABOVE: LILLIAN RUSSELL. Library of Congress

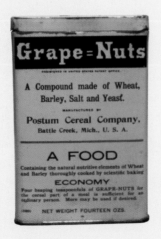

LEFT: C.W. POST CLEARS $385,000 IN 1901 WITH SALES OF HIS GRAPE-NUTS CEREAL AND POSTUM COFFEE SUBSTITUTE. A WHEELER-DEALER WHO IS DOWN ON HIS FINANCIAL LUCK WHEN HE SEEKS HEALTH AT THE KELLOGG SANATORIUM, POST REGAINS HIS FORTUNE BY TURNING MANY OF THE KELLOGG CONCEPTS INTO HIS OWN COMMERCIAL REALITIES. Kraft

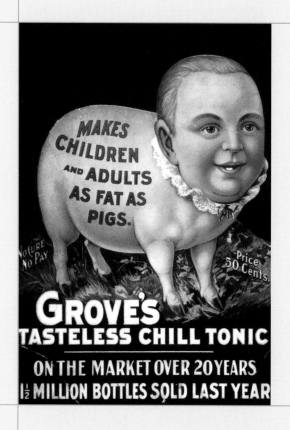

LEFT: Groves Tasteless Chill Tonic, made in St. Louis, not only cures everything, but also adds much-admired heft to the figure.

RIGHT: Maxwell House Coffee took its name from the hotel in Nashville Tenn., where the blend was served and wildly popular. Kraft

RIGHT: Battle Creek, Mich., is the Valhalla of cereal as the new century dawns. Here, packers work in the Kellogg factory in the early 1900s.
Kellogg

cooked. With fewer and fewer servants (they were finding more lucrative work as clerks and telephone operators), this was a boon to house holds. Also, middle-class America was becoming obsessed with germs, a

relatively new term that segued into the science of the era's social reformers. Kellogg's and Post's mass-produced cereals were packaged and so were perceived as cleaner than bulk foods scooped from bins.

Americans had reason to be suspicious of their food supply. The Pure Food and Drug Act was instituted in 1906 after the fallout from the publication of Upton Sinclair's *The Jungle* and its exposure of conditions in Chicago's slaughterhouses.

Home economics came into being because a new class of reformers decided that America would be better off eating by the numbers. Food was viewed as fuel, not fun, and was expected to provide function, not pleasure. Principles of the Industrial Revolution were being applied to the table. (A lot of this thinking hit a positive note with middle-class women who didn't relish more time in the kitchen.)

Another time-saver in the kitchen was the publication of Fanny Merritt Farmer's *Boston Cooking School Cook Book*. Farmer is credited with standardizing measures (instead of instructions like "a knob of butter the size of a hen's egg") and with putting an emphasis on simpler food. "The time is not far distant when knowledge of the principles of diet will be an essential part of one's education," she wrote. "Then mankind will eat to live, will be able to do better mental and physical work and disease will be less frequent."

For most Americans, food was becoming much simpler. The modern way included eating canned goods, gelatin salads, and a breakfast more appropriate for an office worker than for a farmer.

FANNIE FARMER'S
WALDORF SALAD

Apples, finely chopped
Celery finely chopped, plus more for garnish
Mayonnaise
Canned pimentos

Mix EQUAL quantities of finely chopped apple and celery, and moisten with mayonnaise. Garnish with curled celery and canned pimentos cut in strips or fancy shapes. An attractive way of serving this salad is to remove tops from red or green apples, scoop out inside pulp, leaving just enough adhering to skin to keep apples in shape. Refill shells thus made with the salad, replace tops, and serve on lettuce leaves.

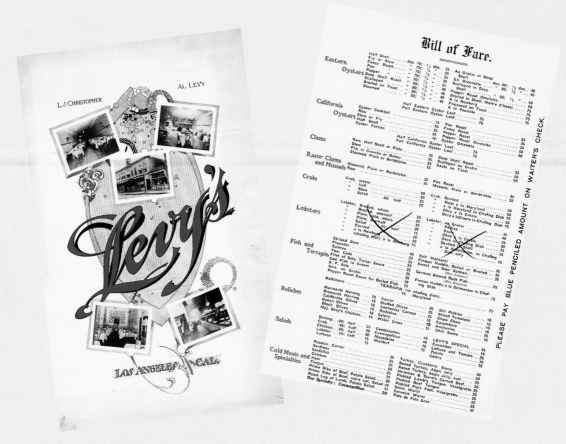

ABOVE: WALDORF SALAD ALREADY MAKES ITS WAY ACROSS THE COUNTRY FROM THE WALDORF-ASTORIA HOTEL IN NEW YORK CITY. FOR 75 CENTS IT COULD BE ORDERED AT LEVY'S IN LOS ANGELES, CALIF. OR, FOR 25 CENTS, DINERS COULD OPT FOR LAMB TONGUE IN VINAIGRETTE. Los Angeles Public Library

ABOVE: ALTHOUGH THE POPULARITY OF HISPANIC FOOD BOOMED AT THE END OF THE CENTURY, IT WAS NO STRANGER TO SOME PARTS OF THE NATION AT THE BEGINNING. ORTEGA BEGAN ITS CHILE CANNING OPERATION IN VENTURA, CALIF., AT THE TAIL END OF THE 1800S, WITH SEEDS BROUGHT IN FROM NEW MEXICO. Ortega

LEFT: THE TIN-BODIED MODEL O IN THIS 1908 PHOTO, HOOVER'S FIRST ELECTRIC SUCTION SWEEPER, WEIGHS 40 POUNDS—AN IMPROVEMENT OVER OTHER "PORTABLE" CLEANERS OF THE DAY THAT WEIGH ALMOST 100 POUNDS. The Hoover Co

RIGHT: TRAIN DINING IS AN ELEGANT AFFAIR IN ITS EARLY YEARS. AIRLINE FOOD WILL FOLLOW SUIT WHEN IT IS INTRODUCED THREE DECADES LATER. Library of Congress

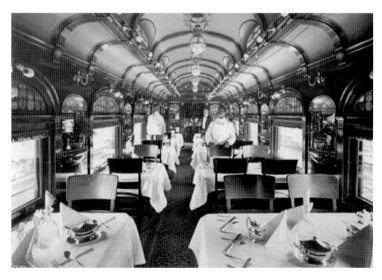

PERFECTION SALAD

[SERVES 6]

2 envelopes unflavored gelatin

1 cup cold water

1½ cups boiling water

½ cup sugar

½ cup vinegar

2 tablespoons lemon juice

1 teaspoon salt

1½ cups finely shredded cabbage

1½ cups chopped celery

¼ cup chopped green bell pepper

¼ cup chopped pimientos, drained

IN LARGE bowl, sprinkle unflavored gelatin over cold water; let stand 1 minute. Add boiling water and stir until gelatin is completely dissolved, about 5 minutes.

Stir in sugar, vinegar, lemon juice, and salt. Chill, stirring occasionally, until mixture is consistency of unbeaten egg whites, about 50 minutes. Fold in remaining ingredients. Turn into 6-cup mold or bowl; chill until firm, about 3 hours.

To serve, unmold onto serving platter and garnish, if desired, with salad greens.

— Knox Gelatin, a booklet of recipes

HERSHEY CHOCOLATE CO. LANCASTER PA. U.S.A.

Hershey's MILK CHOCOLATE.

A NUTRITIOUS CONFECTION.

ABOVE: MILTON HERSHEY INTRODUCES HIS FIRST MILK CHOCOLATE BAR IN 1900 BUT DOESN'T PERFECT HIS FORMULA UNTIL 1905. FOR DECADES THE COMPANY KEEPS THE PRICE AT 5 CENTS— MODIFYING THE SIZE OF THE BAR TO ABSORB RISING OR FALLING COSTS. Hershey Foods

RIGHT: IN 1866
SWISS BUSINESSMAN-
PHARMACIST HENRI
NESTLE INVENTS WHAT
WAS LATER KNOWN AS
INFANT FORMULA. BY
1907 NESTLE WAS A
RECOGNIZED COMPANY
ON BOTH SIDES OF THE
ATLANTIC, WITH AN
AMERICAN PLANT IN
FULTON, N.Y., MAKING
"MILKFOOD" AND
CHOCOLATE. Nestle

OPPOSITE, LOWER RIGHT:
MILTON S. HERSHEY IS
SHOWN WITH A CHILD
FROM THE MILTON
HERSHEY SCHOOL, A
RESIDENTIAL SCHOOL
HE FOUNDED FOR
NEGLECTED BOYS
(AND IN LATER YEARS,
GIRLS). LONG BEFORE
HE DIED, HERSHEY
QUIETLY TRANSFERS
ALL HIS ASSETS TO A
TRUST THAT WOULD
FUND THE SCHOOL.
AT THE END OF THE
CENTURY, EVEN AS A
PUBLICLY TRADED COM-
PANY, ALL HERSHEY'S
PROFITS CONTINUE TO
BENEFIT THE SCHOOL.
Hershey Foods

NESTLE'S FOOD

A BLESSING TO LIFE'S SUNRISE

Infants fed on **Nestle's Food** are strong and robust, because they are well and properly nourished. **Nestle's Food** is easily digested and assimilated, and quickly prepared. It requires the addition of water only (no milk) to prepare it for use.

We want you to prove this for yourself, and wish to send you a free sample of **Nestle's Food,** containing enough for several meals, and our Book for Mothers. Address all letters to

HENRI NESTLE, 73 Warren St., New York.

In answering this advertisement it is desirable that you mention THE PURITAN.

CHICKEN SOUP

[SERVES 8]

Chicken

2 quarts water

½ cup rice, cooked

TAKE THE pieces of chicken not desirable for frying—skin, head and feet—and use giblets. Boil in water until quite tender, skimming well while boiling; remove meat and bones. Have rice ready, and add to the broth. Boil 10 minutes after adding rice and then strain through a wire sieve. Add salt and pepper to taste. This is an excellent broth for the sick, especially one who has bowel trouble.

— From *The C.P. Workers Cook Book*
by the Cumberland Presbyterian Workers
(Canyon City, Texas, 1903)

THE CAMPBELL SOUP CO. ADOPTS RED AND WHITE FOR ITS LABELS AFTER A COMPANY EXECUTIVE ADMIRES CORNELL UNIVERSITY'S FOOTBALL UNIFORMS. APPARENTLY, THE COLORS CATCH THE EYE OF CONSUMERS AS WELL. IN 1904 THE NEW JERSEY COMPANY SELLS MORE THAN 16 MILLION CANS OF SOUP. Campbell Soup Co.

THE BATTLE FOR HEALTH
IN MICHIGAN

They seem so benign now, but just about a century ago, the miracle of breakfast flakes made from corn were drawing some battle lines in Michigan.

America was going through one of its hair-shirt periods—lots of folks feeling free to tell a lot of other folks what they should and shouldn't be eating, should and shouldn't be drinking, should and shouldn't be thinking.

A master at all three categories was Dr. John Harvey Kellogg, recruited to head the Battle Creek Health Institute— a watering hole to which the rich and famous flocked to be poked, deprived and set onto the straight and narrow. Even the seemingly otherwise very level headed Will Rogers was a visitor to the "San."

Much of Dr. Kellogg's thinking was right headed—following the Seventh Day Adventist practices of no alcohol, no tobacco, no meat and no caffeine.

Kellogg, though an accomplished speaker and showman, wasn't much of businessman. Although he had come up with a toasted caramelized cereal product as a substitute for coffee, he had no interest in marketing the product. He went no further with the "granola" he had perfected.

In addition to the sensible diet restrictions, Kellogg has some more stands.

Patients at the San exercsied in athletic diapers, took dunks in electrified pools and were prescribed multiple daily enemas. In fact, Kellogg's philosophy centered on the colon and one of his tenets was that "A housebroken colon is a broken colon."

Then C.W. Post entered the picture. A patient at the San, he claimed that the nine-month regimen he survived there changed his life. He offered to go into business with Kellogg, marketing the food products the San serves—and for $50 a week, he'll also pray over the health facilities guests.

Dr. Kellogg was determinded to be the only rooster on the San's walk. In a huff, Post went across town, opened his own sanitarium and introduced Postum and GrapeNuts cereal. You be the judge of where the formulas came from. Cereal titans have been arguing the issue for a century.

Luckily (or not) Dr. Kellogg's brother W.K. Kellogg stepped up to the plate. What the elder Dr. Kellogg had in charisma, the younger Mr. Kellogg had in business sense. He saw Post becoming a millionaire on concepts his brother had been preaching for years.

No sentimental fool, W.K. waited until his brother was out of the country to make his move. He bought up controlling shares in the floundering Kellogg Co. and soon thereafter, another cereal fortune was made.

The first act ended on a karmic note. C.W. Post committed suicide in 1914, victim of a post-operative depression. The Kellogg boys both lived to the ripe old age of 91.

RIGHT: After dinner, the well-heeled patrons paid for the priv-
iledge of performing the mandatory walk on the roof of the "San"
for exercise. Willard Public Library

LADY BALTIMORE CAKE

[SERVES 12]

CAKE
½ cup butter

1½ cups sugar

1 cup water

3 cups flour

2 teaspoons baking powder

4 stiffly beaten egg whites

1 teaspoon vanilla

CREAM BUTTER and sugar, adding water gradually. Then add flour and baking powder. Fold in stiffly beaten egg whites and vanilla. Bake in 3 buttered cake pans in 375-degree oven until layers test done.

FILLING
1½ cups sugar

½ cup water

2 stiffly beaten egg whites

BOIL SUGAR and water in double boiler until syrup forms a thread. Beat well and pour slowly over egg whites. Beat until mixture may be spread on cakes.

FILLING
½ cup raisins

5 diced figs

½ cup chopped pecans

⅓ cup candied cherries

SPRINKLE RAISINS, figs, pecans, and cherries on the cakes. Stack layers.

2 cups sugar

½ cup water

2 stiffly beaten egg whites

1 teaspoon vanilla

BOIL SUGAR and water in double boiler until syrup forms a thread. Beat well and pour slowly over beaten egg whites and vanilla. Beat until mixture may be spread on cakes. Spread completely over layered cake.

This cake was featured in Owen Wister's book *Lady Baltimore*, written in 1906. Several stories exist about the origins of the cake, but it is often credited to the managers of the Charleston, S.C., Lady Baltimore Tea Room. Wister is better known at the end of the century as the author of *The Virginian*.

ABOVE: HOUSEWIFE MELITTA BENTZ INVENTS THE DRIP COFFEEMAKER IN 1907 USING A SHEET OF HER SON'S SCHOOL BLOTTING PAPER AS A FILTER. Melitta

Upon the tide of Time's Eternal Sea
A new-born year is wafted to our shore.
From out the darkness of eternity,
A century's dawn breaks on the world once more.

Begin the New Century Right. Scientific opinion everywhere agrees that excessive meat eating is not only extravagant, but positively injurious. Health, happiness, temper and temperament largely depend upon the character and quality of the food.

The benefit of an increased use of cereal foods is constantly being demonstrated by scientific research and testified to by millions of intelligent people who have discovered by experience that "more Quaker Oats and less meat" not only makes them feel better, but also that it is a far more appetizing and palatable diet.

Quaker Oats MUFFINS

EAT MORE Quaker Oats LESS MEAT

At all Grocers in 2-lb. Packages.

QUAKER OATS makes not only the best breakfast porridge in the world, but also delicious, wholesome bread, muffins, cakes, soups and puddings. Write for our *Cereal Cook Book*, edited by Mrs. Rorer, Sent Free, postpaid.

The American Cereal Co.,   Monadnock Building, Chicago, Ill.

Short-sighted man—lacks penetration.

He is a short-sighted man indeed who cannot see the other end of the medical breakfast food habit. Any food that coddles digestion all the time must weaken digestion at last by sheer lack of exercise.

A strong digestion might not be greatly weakened by a diet of rich foods,—but even the strongest digestion cannot withstand the weakening effects of laboratory foods.

Only a short-sighted man will deny that natural digestion must be relied on after all for assimilation of the food elements which the body demands,—and the better the digestion the better the prospect of health. The way to preserve the strength of natural digestion is to offer it only natural food.

The one natural food that fills every need of body and nerve and brain,—that gives every food element in exactly the proportions demanded by the human system,—is

Quaker Oats

No other food has ever been granted that steadfast favor in which Quaker Oats is held at a million well-served breakfast tables.

You'll see the reason, unless you are

A SHORT-SIGHTED MAN.

LEFT AND ABOVE: THE QUAKER OATS CO. IS INCORPORATED IN 1901, BUT THE FIRM HAS BEEN OPERATING AS THE AMERICAN CEREAL CO. SINCE 1888. THE TRADEMARK, "THE FIGURE OF A MAN IN QUAKER GARB," IS THE FIRST FOR A BREAKFAST CEREAL, REGISTERED IN 1877. QUAKER'S PACKAGING, TOO, IS INNOVATIVE: INSTEAD OF SCOOPING FROM BARRELS, CONSUMERS COULD BUY INDIVIDUAL PACKAGES. Photo in upper left: Quaker Oats Co.

Ohio chocolatier Clarence Crane introduces a new candy in 1912. In playing around with formulas to come up with a sweet to sell during the warm, unairconditioned summer months. He called the candy with a hole in the middle LifeSavers in honor of the safety devices just coming into vogue on ocean liners. The first flavor is Pep-O-Mint. Crane sells the rights to the candy to Edward Noble for $2,900 and it's Noble who comes up with the tin foil wrappers to keep the candy fresh. In the 1930s, LifeSavers were touted as a theater snack. In the 1950s, they were advertised as an affordable treat. And like every American candy worth its sugar, LifeSavers had a war role.

Dessert in Motion

One of the century's most enduring food products is a silly, bouncy shimmer of a thing called Jell-O. In 1845, Peter Cooper patents a sweet product that is set with gelatin. And in 1890 Charles B. Knox patents Knox gelatin, perfect for oh-so-popular savory aspics.

But it is carpenter Pearle B. Wait, playing pharmaceutical inventor with cough and laxative formulas, who in 1897 comes up with the fruit-flavored gelatin that is the backbone of Jell-O. (He had hoped that gelatin would serve as a thickening agent and the fruit flavor would make the medicines more palatable.) It is Wait's wife, May, who comes up with the Jell-O name.

ABOVET: JELL-O'S 1908 PACKAG-
ING FOR RASPBERRY, ONE OF THE
ORIGINAL FLAVORS. Kraft

But what Wait has in chemistry, he lacks in commercial moxie. In 1899 he sells his formula to orator Frank Woodward for $450. Woodward knows his way around distribution. In 1896 he buys the patent for Grain-O, a roasted cereal coffee "for those who can't drink tea and coffee." It is the coffee substitute that made enough money to carry Jell-O along until the new dessert replaces Grain-O as a moneymaker.

In 1900 the Jell-O name is first used by Woodward's Genesee Pure Food Co. The advertising campaign proves so successful that in 1902 Jell-O sales mount to $250,000. In 1909 the Genesee Pure Food Company posts sales earnings of more than one million.

In 1925, the (renamed for its star performer) Jell-O Co. is acquired by Postum Cereal Co. Not a company to let its laurels slide, it continued its Jell-O innovations. In 1952 the company introduces D-Zerta, a sugar-free gelatin, to retail markets. (The product had been available in health food stores and institutions since 1923.) In the 1950s the company branches out to the pudding market.

When Jell-O sales slide in the 1960s and 1970s (America's new food sophistication can probably be blamed), Jell-O introduces a line of flavors for salads, concoctions like celery, seasoned tomato, mixed vegetable, and Italian. Those flavors don't take with consumers, although they have been congealing savory salads since 1905 and the introduction of breakthrough Perfection Salad recipe.

But not to worry. By the time Jell-O celebrates its 100th anniversary (marked with a "champagne" flavor Jell-O), the company has introduced already-jelled Jell-O Gelatin Snacks for harried mothers who couldn't wait thirty minutes for the powder and water to set. The company has also developed Jell-O Jigglers, bouncy cut-out and molded shapes that call for double the amount of Jell-O in the recipe. Smart thinking there.

And then there are the college kids who are sucking down Jell-O shots, a concoction that uses vodka in place of cold water in the recipe.

RIGHT: JELL-O TURNS
100 YEARS OLD WITH A
LIMITED EDITION
FLAVOR. Kraft

It's Here!

the new low-calorie gelatin

D-ZERTA

...the sweet dessert that's sugar-free!

Try the new gelatin dessert D-ZERTA—in the six delicious Jell-O flavors, delightfully sweetened with saccharin, and containing *only 10 calories per serving!* (Sugar-sweetened gelatins have up to 85 calories a serving!) D-Zerta's entirely carbohydrate free! So, if your physician recommends a low-calorie or sugar-free diet, you can *still* enjoy tempting desserts and sparkling salads *at a cost of only 4¢ to 5¢ a serving* with low-calorie, sugar-free D-Zerta. Complete nutrition information plus appetizing recipes with every package. Look for D-Zerta in the diet-foods section of your food store *today!*

A Product of General Foods

MADE BY THE MAKERS OF JELL-O DESSERTS

Made by the makers of **JELL-O**

1900: Baltimore-based McCormick & Co. is already a force. Founded in 1889 by twenty-five-year-old Willoughby M. McCormick, the first products are root beer, flavoring extracts, and fruit syrups and juices. The product line grows to include witch hazel, cold cream, sulphur, epsom salts, castor oil, food colors, cream of tartar, and tooth powder. In 1896 McCormick acquires a Philadelphia spice company and has all the equipment shipped to Baltimore so the company could expand into the spice trade.

1900: The kitchen range is redesigned to burn coal instead of wood. Even in city apartments, many cooks are still cooking in fireplaces.

1900: Wesson Oil is introduced.

1900: A vendor at the Ringling Bros. and Barnum & Bailey Circus develops a snack of caramelized sugar that he twists with a fork to make threads. He sells his patent to a candy machine operation, which names the confection "fairy floss candy" and sells it at the

1904 St. Louis World's Fair. By the 1920s, the festival treat is known as cotton candy.

1900: Heinz has been putting up fifty-seven varieties of pickles near Sharpsburg, Pa., since 1869.

1900: Ninety-five percent of all flour sold in the United States is bought by individuals for home cooking.

Campbell's Soup Co.

1900: Dr. John Thomas Dorrance, an M.I.T.-trained chemist, earns a Gold Medallion for excellence at the Paris Exposition. He has found a simple solution for a manufacturing problem and will turn it into a fortune for the Campbell Soup Co.

At the turn of the century, America isn't a big soup-eating nation. For one, soup takes time to make, and with most stoves still fueled by wood, it is an expensive as well as a time-consuming operation. And second, it isn't a big part of American culinary tradition. (One historian has attributed that to Americans' innate sense of individualism: instead of the communal pot, they want distinct elements on their plates—a meat, a vegetable, and a starch.)

Individual or not, Dorrance travels abroad and earns his doctorate in Germany. And he has come to love soup. But canned soup, he knows, is expensive. (His uncle runs the Joseph Campbell Preserve Co., so he has some insight into the subject.) Soup is heavy and bulky, making it onerous to transport. For that reason, only two companies specialize in soup at the end of the 19th century.

Dorrance figures that if the cans are smaller, they'd be less expensive to ship. So he removes most of the heaviest ingredient—the water. He then ships smaller cans of stronger soup that the housewife could dilute.

His first five flavors, for no particular reason, are tomato, consommé, vegetable, chicken, and oxtail. By 1905 the company sells a line of 21 flavors.

1901: James Dole, cousin of Hawaii (a U.S. territory) governor Sanford Dole, begins growing pineapple on 60 acres on Wahiawa, north of Oahu. James Dole, fresh out of Harvard University, first considers growing coffee, but instead invests his $1,200 in pineapple. With his success, Americans will associate Hawaii with pineapple throughout the century. "Hawaii-style" on menus and in recipes begins to be synonymous with "includes pineapple."

1901: A frankfurter in a hot bun is served at the New York Polo Grounds. A star is born.

1902: Eight percent of U.S. homes have electricity provided by power stations.

1902: Nabisco introduces Barnum's Animal Crackers. The crackers appear just before Christmas in boxes topped with white string so they can be hung from Christmas trees.

1902: Karo Corn Syrup debuts.

1902: The first Automat opens in Philadelphia. But it is in New York City (where the first one opened in 1912) that the concept of the large, white-tiled restaurants with food delivered through coin-operated doors really catches on. (The last Automat closed in 1991. A glass door facade of an original Automat is in the Smithsonian Institution.)

1902: Pepsi-Cola Co. is founded.

1902: Fannie Farmer opens her own cooking school in Boston.

1903: Chili is introduced to the north by a group of Texans at the Chicago World Fair. It is dispensed at a pavilion named San Antonio Chiley Stand.

1903: Ambrose W. Straub patents a machine for making peanut butter.

1903: A San Pedro, Calif., packer puts tuna fish into cans and begins a major industry.

1904: The hamburger, one version of the story goes, is introduced at the Universal Exposition in St. Louis, Mo. The exposition is also credited with being the birthplace of iced tea and hot dogs. More likely, these creations have been regional for years, but did not have a high national profile.

1904: Another hit at the 1904 St. Louis fair is peanut butter. C.H. Sumner sold $705.11 of the treat at his concession stand.

In 1890 a St. Louis physician supposedly encourages the owner of a food products company, George A. Bayle Jr., to process and package ground peanut paste as a protein substitute for people with poor teeth who can't chew meat. Bayle begins selling peanut butter out of barrels for about six cents per pound.

Dr. John Harvey Kellogg also experiments with peanut butter as a vegetarian source of protein for his patients. His brother, W.K. Kellogg, is business manager of their sanatorium, the Western Health Reform Institute, but soon opens Sanitas Nut Co. to produce products like peanut butter to local grocery stores. The Kelloggs' patent for the "Process of Preparing Nut Meal" in 1895 describes "a pasty adhesive substance that is for convenience of distinction termed nut butter."

1904: Campbell's Pork & Beans are introduced.

1905: Galatoire's opens in New Orleans.

1905: A dinner at Delmonico's is in celebration of Mark Twain's seventieth birthday, and 172 writers attend to honor the master.

1905: The country's first pizzeria opens in New York, but it won't be until soldiers return from World War II that the pies really take off.

1905: Tootsie Rolls are manufactured in a four-story factory in New York City. Immigrant Leo Hirshfield brought the recipe from Austria and first makes the chocolate rolls in a small shop. He names the candy after his daughter, whose nickname is Tootsie. The Tootsie Roll is the first penny candy to be individually wrapped.

1905: Royal Crown Cola is conceived and bottled in Columbus, Ga.

1905: Jelly beans are first advertised in the *Chicago Daily News* at nine cents a pound.

1906: The hot fudge sundae is born at C.C. Brown's ice cream parlor in Hollywood.

1906: The U.S. Pure Food and Drug Act passes.

ABOVE: NOT ONLY DO WORKERS USE MANUAL SCALES TO WEIGH 2½-POUND BOXES OF HERSHEY KISSES, EACH KISS IS WRAPPED BY HAND IN ITS TIN-FOIL PAPER. THE WORKERS, ALL WOMEN, ARE PAID BY THE NUMBER OF PIECES THEY WRAP. Hershey Foods

1906: Kelloggs introduces Kelloggs Corn Flakes.

1906: Soda companies begin an advertising battle that is to last the century. The first ad to use Dr Pepper's first slogan and mascot is painted on a Waco, Texas, building. The King of Beverages is hawked by a grand lion promoting "vim, vigor, and vitality."

1906: The hot dog gets its name from cartoonist Tad Dorgan who draws Germans as dachshunds.

1907: A slim figure is still considered a mark of ill health, with patent medicines that promise a remedy for the thin outnumbering those that promise weight loss. Actress Lillian Russell, considered the beauty of her time, weighs almost 200 pounds.

1907: Hershey's Kisses are introduced. The paper "plume" is added to the product wrapper in 1921 to distinguish the Hershey product as the original. In 1924, Hershey establishes a trademark for the paper insert. Kisses are made continuously except during World War II, when foil is rationed.

1907: Minnesota Valley Canning Co. in Le Sueur begins packing peas as well as corn.

1907: Scott rolls out paper towels. The product is introduced as a way to lessen spreading germs in schools.

1908: Post Toasties Corn Flakes are introduced.

1908: Hershey introduces almonds into its Hershey Chocolate Bar. The bar is introduced in 1900, but Hershey continues to change the formula and isn't satisfied until 1905. Milton Hershey, with only a fourth-grade education and several career failures, has made a success of the Lancaster Caramel Co. he founded in Pennsylvania.

1908: Half of all Americans live on the country's 6 million farms or in towns of fewer than 2,500 people.

1908: The Dixie Cup, one of the first paper cups, is produced in New York.

1908: Chicago imposes the first U.S. law making the pasteurization of milk mandatory unless it comes from tuberculin-tested cows.

1908: Tea bags are pioneered by New York tea and coffee wholesaler Thomas Sullivan. He ships samples of his blends to customers in small muslin or China silk bags. Customers find they can brew tea by merely pouring boiling water over the bag in a cup; they place hundreds of orders.

1908: Long an American favorite, ketchup is first commercially processed by the F. & J. Heinz Co. in 1876.

1908: Melitta Benz, a German hausfrau, punctures the bottom of a tin cup and lines it with her son's school blotter paper to make a contraption to filter coffee's bitter grounds. By 1937 the fast-drip filter cone and its conical paper insert is introduced. The product is introduced to the United States in 1964.

1909: Coca-Cola is exported to Britain for the first time.

1909: Chemist Leo Baekeland develops Bakelite, the world's first polymer. The plastic material does not transmit heat, and it will become popular as a safe kitchen pots and cooking appliance handles.

1909: Milton Hershey opens the Milton Hershey School, a home and school for orphaned and neglected boys.

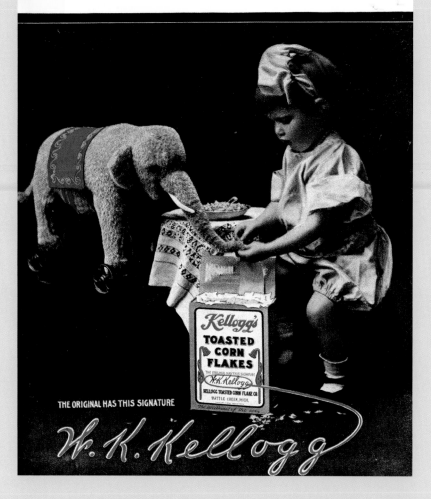

"I Eat It by the Trunk-full too"

Kellogg's TOASTED CORN FLAKES

THE ORIGINAL HAS THIS SIGNATURE

W. K. Kellogg

THE 1910S BEGAN with a roar and ended with a whimper—a tempestuous decade of high living, high prices, the introduction of income taxes, women's suffrage, World War I, an influenza pandemic that killed between 20 million and 50 million people, and, as if to put a lid on this Pandora's box, Prohibition.

America's economy was chugging along, having evolved from agrarian to industrial. Immigration was at full throttle. The number of servants, who often came from the newly arrived masses, continued to decline as immigrants found jobs in newly minted factories and mines.

Through the end of the decade, the number of domestic servants dropped from 1.8 million to 1.4 million while the number of households rose from 20.3 million to 24.4 million. This meant homemakers, once the managing directors of housework, became responsible for the hands-on duty. But industry was there to offer a helping hand. This was the decade that saw the first

LEFT: MASS MARKETING MAY HAVE JUST BEGUN, BUT COMPANIES ARE ALREADY REALIZING THE COMPETITIVE EDGE A BRAND NAME COULD BRING. DESPITE THE SWEET MESSAGE OF THE CHILD WITH HER STUFFED ELEPHANT, KELLOGG IS POINTEDLY SAYING THAT ITS PRODUCT IS THE ORIGINAL, NOT THE CORN FLAKES SOLD BY THE C. W. POST CO. Kellogg's

big introduction of household appliances.

But all was not progress. A depression in 1914–1915 led the nutrition reformers, the eat-by-the-numbers zealots of the previous decade, to poke their noses into the eating habits of immigrants and the poor. Concern was valid; many immigrants lived in cramped quarters in large Eastern cities where there was a lot of disease. But food was one area where a little knowledge could be a dangerous thing.

One system of judging malnutrition, the Dumferline Scale, ranked height, weight, eyesight, breathing, muscularity, mental alertness, and rosiness of complexion as benchmarks of health. This worked fine for British and German children, but was inappropriate for the olive skin of many Italians, Jews, Greeks, and Turks. In the hands of officials convinced of widespread malnutrition, the school lunch program ballooned, but the American food ideal wasn't necessarily that of the immigrant's.

Italian immigrant John Fante recognized the two worlds of his food. "At the lunch hour I huddle over my lunch pail, for my mother doesn't wrap my sandwiches in wax paper and she makes them too large and the lettuce leaves protrude. Worse, the bread is homemade; not

ABOVE: IMMIGRANTS ARE CHECKED FOR DISEASE AT ELLIS ISLAND BEFORE BEING ALLOWED INTO THE UNITED STATES.
California Museum of Photography UC/Riverside

sugar

1- none on fruits
2- none in desserts
3- less on cereals
4- less in coffee & tea
5- less in preserving
6- less cake & candy
7- use other sweeteners

save it

UNITED STATES FOOD ADMINISTRATION

LEFT: REFINED SUGAR CONSUMPTION EXPLODES IN THE U.S., BUT AS THE NATION ENTERS WORLD WAR I, THE UNITED STATES FOOD ADMINISTRATION ENCOURAGES CONSERVATION.
Library of Congress

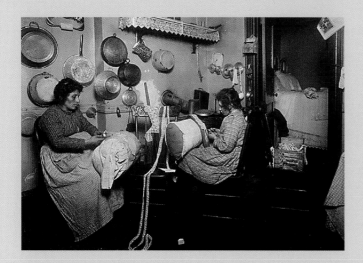

bakery bread, not 'American' bread. I make a great fuss because I can't have mayonnaise and other 'American' things," Fante recalled in *American Mercury* magazine in the 1930s.

And Fante's family no doubt drank wine with its meals—unlike nonimmigrant families. But that, too, was about to change.

Secretary of State William Jennings Bryan, a Prohibitionist, served Welch's grape juice instead of wine at a 1913 dinner for the British ambassador. The next year, Secretary of the Navy Josephus Daniels ordered that the navy's traditional rum grog be replaced with Welch's grape juice.

By 1919 the Temperance League had won out and the sale and distribution of alcohol was banned. In 1920 saloons were shuttered and distilleries closed, and America would begin its Noble Experiment.

ABOVE: IN THIS 1911 PHOTOGRAPH, AN ILLITERATE WOMAN AND HER THIRTEEN-YEAR-OLD DAUGHTER ARE IN THEIR NEW YORK CITY TENEMENT MAKING LACE FOR PILLOWS. Library of Congress, Lewis W. Hine, Photographer

RIGHT: FIVE-YEAR-OLD MANUEL IS A SHRIMP AND OYSTER PICKER IN BILOXI, MISS. WHO LIKE MANY OF HIS PEERS, WILL NEVER SEE A SCHOOL. Library of Congress, Lewis W. Hine, Photographer

ABOVE: Before Milton Hershey gets his national brand of candy into grocery stores, newsstands, and other outlets, all candy is sold in candy stores like this one, the Palace of Sweets in Seattle, Wash. Chocolate isn't sold in the summer, melting as it does in the heat.

RIGHT: The arrival of tinned cheese is a revelation for homes without refrigeration.
Kraft

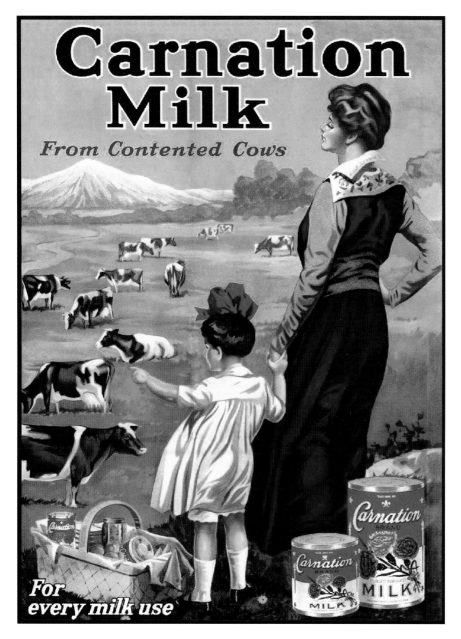

LEFT AND BELOW: JOHN BAPTIST MEYENBERG CAME UP WITH AN IDEA TO PROCESS CANNED EVAPORATED MILK IN 1866. HIS EMPLOYERS AT THE ANGLO-SWISS CONDENSED MILK WERE DOING QUITE WELL MAKING SWEETENED CONDENSED MILK, SO HIS SUGGESTION WAS REJECTED. MEYENBERG IMMIGRATED TO THE UNITED STATES AND BEGAN HIS OWN COMPANY, HELVETIA MILK CONDENSING CO. (PET MILK), EVENTUALLY MARKETING UNSWEETENED CONDENSED MILK IN 1890.

ALTHOUGH BORDEN RECEIVED HIS PATENT IN 1854, UNSWEETENED CONDENSED MILK WAS NOT SUCCESS-FULLY CANNED UNTIL 1885 BY COMPETITOR MEYENBERG. BORDEN ADDED EVAPORATED MILK TO THE PRODUCT LINE IN 1892.

AMERCIA WAS READY. CHUCK WAGON COOKS LOVE THE STUFF FOR MAKING GRAVY, MOTHERS WITHOUT REFRIGERATION LIKED HAVING IT IN THE PANTRY AND AS THE UNION FORCES HAD DISCOVERED, IT WAS A GREAT RATON TO TAKE ALONG FOR THE TROOPS. Nestle

ABOVE: THE IMMIGRANT INFLUENCE IS FELT FAR BEYOND THE COUNTRY'S PORT CITIES. THE O.B. MACARONI FACTORY IN FORT WORTH, TEXAS, IS IN FULL SWING BY 1914. IN FACT, WITH WORLD WAR I, COMES LIMITATIONS ON IMPORTS SUCH AS PASTA AND AMERICA LEARNS TO MAKE ITS OWN. O B Macaroni

ABOVE: COKE IS THE "PAUSE THAT REFRESHES" IN THIS 1912 POSTER. The Coca-Cola Company

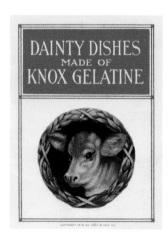

GREEN CORN, CREOLE STYLE

[Serves 4]

4 tablespoons butter

2 tablespoons chopped green bell pepper

4 tablespoons flour

1 cup tomato soup

1 teaspoon salt

1 tablespoon onion juice

1 tablespoon chopped parsley

2 cups corn kernels cut from cob

MELT BUTTER and cook pepper in it until tender. Add flour, blend, and add tomato soup. Stir until smooth. Add seasonings and corn, heat thoroughly, and serve at once.

— Campbell's

FRENCH CHERRY DRESSING

[Yields about ⅓ cup]

½ teaspoon salt

¼ teaspoon pepper

2 tablespoons olive oil

2 teaspoons vinegar

2 tablespoons maraschino cherry juice

2 or 3 maraschino cherries, mashed fine

COMBINE ALL ingredients and stir thoroughly before pouring over lettuce.

— *White House Cook Book* by Hugo Ziemann and Mrs. F. L. Gillette (Saalfield Publishing, 1924)

KITCHEN GIRLS   T.I.S.   BRADY

LEFT: STUDENTS AT THE U.S.
GOVERNMENT-OPERATED
TULALIP INDIAN SCHOOL IN
WASHINGTON RAISE MOST OF
THE SCHOOL'S FOOD ON THE
GROUNDS AND PREPARE IT IN
THE KITCHEN. MRS. RYMAN,
THE COOK, SUPERVISES BREAD
BAKING IN THIS 1912 SCENE.
IDENTIFIED WORKERS ARE
LAURA WILBUR (SWINOMISH,
KNEELING AT LEFT), JULIA
ABBOTT (LUMMI, SECOND FROM
LEFT), CATHERINE EDWARDS
(SWINOMISH), AND ISABELLA
LOUKE (MUCKLESHOOT).
Museum of History & Industry, Seattle: Ferdinand Brady,
Photographer

RIGHT: MOST BAKING IS
STILL DONE IN THE HOME,
AND FLOUR IS BOUGHT IN
BULK. Pioneer

ABOVE: GENERAL
ELECTRIC RANGES ARE
DELIVERED TO TYLER,
TEXAS, IN 1916.
Schenectady Museum

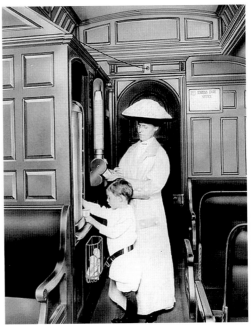

RIGHT: PAPER-CUP
DISPENSERS ON TRAINS
PROMISE THE END OF
SHARING LADLES AS WELL
AS GERMS. Hugh Moore Dixie Cup
Company Collection, David Bishop Skillman
Library, Lafayette College

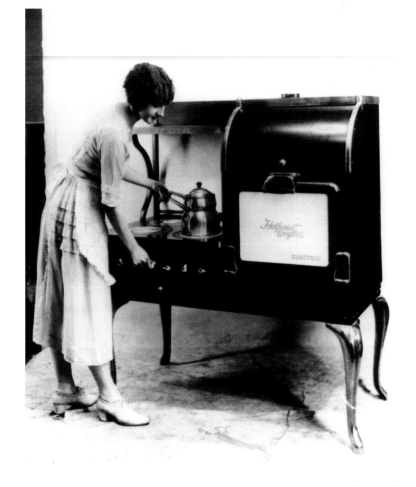

LEFT: In 1915, Alfred Mellowes invented the first electric self-contained refrigerator. In 1918, he sells the company to the president of the General Motors Corp. the company becomes Michigan Frigidaire. This, a wood enclosed unit, is the original model. Frigidaire

RIGHT: Stoves, like women, got legs at the beginning of the century. Lifting the appliance off of the floor made the kitchen far easier to clean and showcased that clean floor for all to see. Sanitation was next to godliness in these technologically advanced kitchens of American homes.

LUNCHEON ASPARAGUS

[SERVES 4–6]

2 bunches asparagus
4 tablespoons butter
1 cup soft bread crumbs
2 hard-boiled eggs, sliced
Pimento, for garnish

WASH AND scrape asparagus. Tie in small bundles and cook in boiling, salted water with heads out for 15 minutes. Put heads under water and cook for 10 minutes. Drain and arrange on a hot platter.

Remove strings.

Melt butter and fry bread crumbs to a pale straw color. Sprinkle over asparagus. Arrange egg slices around asparagus, garnish with strips of pimento, and serve at once.

— *White House Cook Book*

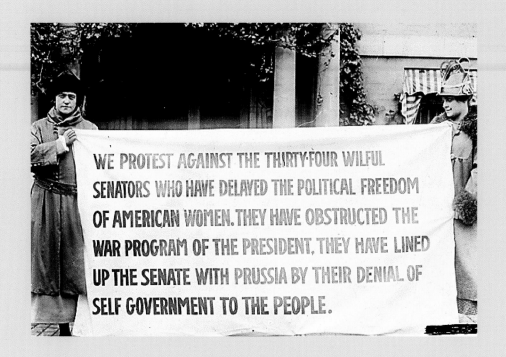

OPPOSITE, ABOVE, RIGHT:
SUFFRAGISTS PARADE IN
THE STREETS OF THEIR
TOWNS, PICKET THE WHITE
HOUSE, AND LOBBY THEIR
REPRESENTATIVES IN
CONGRESS TO OBTAIN THE
RIGHT TO VOTE. Library of Congress

PIGGLY WIGGLY, A
SOUTHERN GROCERY, IS
CREDITED WITH CREATING
A FULL-SERVICE STORE
WITH MEAT AND PRODUCE
AND PANTRY ITEMS, THE
FIRST SUPERMARKET. THIS
IS THE MEMPHIS STORE AT
THE END OF THE DECADE.
Piggly Wiggly Co.

POTATO
CARAMEL CAKE
[SERVES 10–12]

2 cups light brown sugar

4 eggs, separated

⅔ cup shortening

½ cup milk

3 squares baker's chocolate, melted

1 cup hot potatoes, cubed

2 cups all purpose flour, divided

½ teaspoon salt

2 teaspoons baking powder

1 teaspoon cloves

1 teaspoon cinnamon

2 teaspoons nutmeg

1 cup chopped nuts, floured

FILLING / FROSTING

1 cup half-and-half cream

½ cup butter

2 cups brown sugar

1 teaspoon vanilla

CREAM SUGAR, egg yolks, and shortening; add milk, then melted chocolate beaten in while hot, and the cubed potatoes. Reserve ¼ cup flour, add rest of flour, salt, baking powder, and spices sifted together; fold in floured nuts and stiffly beaten egg whites. Pour into greased and floured cake pans and bake at 375 degrees for 20 minutes.

To make filling, cook cream, butter, and sugar together until it forms a soft ball in cold water. Remove from fire, add vanilla, and beat until creamy. When cool, spread between layers and on top.

— *Bewley's Best* recipe pamphlet

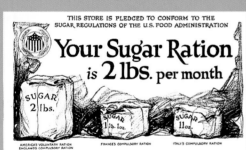

THIS STORE IS PLEDGED TO CONFORM TO THE
SUGAR REGULATIONS OF THE U.S. FOOD ADMINISTRATION

Your Sugar Ration
is **2 lbs.** per month

SUGAR 2 lbs.

SUGAR 1 lb. 1 oz.

SUGAR 11 oz.

AMERICA'S VOLUNTARY RATION
ENGLAND'S COMPULSORY RATION

FRANCE'S COMPULSORY RATION

ITALY'S COMPULSORY RATION

We must confine our consumption of Sugar
to not more than 2 lbs. per person per month
in order to provide a restricted ration
to England, France and Italy.

FOR EVERY FIGHTER
A WOMAN WORKER

Y·W·C·A·

BACK OUR SECOND LINE OF DEFENSE
UNITED WAR WORK CAMPAIGN

WOMEN!
HELP AMERICA'S SONS
WIN THE WAR

BUY
U.S. GOVERNMENT BONDS
2ND LIBERTY LOAN
OF 1917

Remember Your First Thrill of
AMERICAN LIBERTY

YOUR DUTY-Buy
United States Government Bonds
2nd Liberty Loan of 1917

The Fruits of Victory

Write for Free Book to
National War Garden Commission
Washington, D.C.
Charles Lathrop Pack, President   P.S. Ridsdale, Secretary

ABOVE: THE PRESIDENT OF THE
NATIONAL WAR GARDEN COMMISSION
HAD AN APT NAME. INDEED, PACKING
THE FRUIT AND VEGETABLES OF THE
GARDEN IS GRUELING BUSINESS IN
THE DAYS BEFORE AIR-CONDITIONING.
THIS MIGHT HAVE BEEN ONE OF THE
STRONGEST CLUES TO WORKING WOMEN
THAT SOMETHING WAS AMISS IN
BOTH WORKING AND KEEPING A
HOME. Library of Congress

RIGHT: NOT FOR THE LAST TIME
DURING THE 20TH CENTURY,
MANUFACTURERS ENLIST THE HELP OF
HOME-FRONT WOMEN IN THE WAR
EFFORT. Alltrista Corp.

DOING LAUNDRY IS ITSELF A TWO-DAY AFFAIR. FIRST WATER HAS TO BE BOILED—ON A CAST IRON STOVE THAT MUST BE BLACKENED AND POLISHED ONCE A WEEK. THEN THE SOAPS AND CLEANING AGENTS ARE ASSEMBLED FROM AN INVENTORY THAT INCLUDES BORAX, TURPENTINE, AMMONIA, AND WASHING POWDER. (BY THE 1920S, HOUSEWIVES COULD PURCHASE MANUFACTURED CLEANERS AND POLISHES; BEFORE THEN IT WAS YET SOMETHING ELSE THEY HAD TO MAKE.)

IRONING—USING SEVEN-POUND IRONS THAT ARE HEATED ON THE STOVE—TAKES UP THE SECOND DAY.

THE ARRIVAL OF MECHANICAL HELP IS HEAVEN SENT. AN ITEM AS MUNDANE AS A PORCELAIN RANGE—NO MORE BLACKENING, NO MORE POLISHING—REMOVES ONE TWO-HOUR CHORE.

THE APPLIANCES OF THE TIMES, IN KEEPING WITH THE NEW AWARENESS OF GERMS AND SANITATION, ARE SET ON LEGS, WHICH ALLOW FOR EASIER CLEANING.

1910: Seventy percent of U.S. bread is baked at home, down from eighty percent in 1890. Processors employ more than 68,000 people to can 3 billion cans of food per year.

1910: The first refrigerated tank car for wine brings California wine to the East, but most Golden State wine is shipped in oak barrels by steamer around Cape Horn.

1911: The first canned chili and tamales are produced in San Antonio by William Gebhardt. The term "tamale pie" first appears in print.

1911: Procter & Gamble introduces Crisco, the first solid vegetable shortening. The product is a hard sell for women who had been taught to cook with butter and lard. To promote its product, the manufacturer suggests glazing sweet potatoes with brown sugar and Crisco, and spreading sandwiches with Crisco mixed with an egg yolk, Worcester-shire sauce, lemon juice, and vinegar. Orthodox Jews, however, love the shortening because it is neither meat nor dairy, so it can be used at any kosher meal. Crisco has better sales late in the decade, when lard and butter become scarce because of the war effort.

1911: Electric chafing dishes, skillets, grills, toasters, percolators, and waffle irons are introduced at the New York Electric Exhibition. More uses for that new in-house electricity.

1911: Morton adds magnesium carbonate (an anti-caking agent) to its table salt to create a product that flows freely, particularly in damp weather. (The additive used later is calcium silicate.) It is introduced in 1912.

1912: Ohio chocolate manufacturer Clarence Crane develops peppermint candy LifeSavers as a summer candy, which can withstand heat better than chocolate can. The next year he sells the rights to Edward Noble for $2,900. Noble develops tin-foil wrappers to keep the mints fresh (they had been packaged in cardboard rolls).

1912: Nabisco introduces Oreo Biscuits to compete with the Hydrox biscuit bonbons rolled out in 1910.

1912: Immigrants pour into the country. Between 1910 and 1924, 12 million come through Ellis Island. All are examined for health problems; two percent are sent back across the Atlantic. Meanwhile, 1 million emigrate from Mexico during 1910–1930. Many of these immigrants have large families and are desperately poor, leading to abusive child labor.

1912: New York deli owner Richard Hellmann begins packing his mayonnaise in glass jars. The product is such a success that he gives up the deli in 1915 and devotes his energy to manufacturing.

1912: The first Whitman Sampler appears, complete with an identifying chart inside the lid.

1913: General Electric markets toasters, irons, and an electric range.

1914: The first electric refrigerator is introduced for commercial use, but it's not until after World War I that the miracle machines are widely available. By 1937 more than 2 million American households have new refrigerators.

1914: Campbell's promotes its soups as recipe ingredients to help much-burdened homemakers.

1914: Lettuce, asparagus, watermelons, cantaloupes, and tomatoes grown in California's irrigated fields are transported 3,000 miles away in refrigerated railcars.

1914: George Washington Carver's experiments prove the value of peanuts and sweet potatoes in replenishing soil fertility.

1914: The Reuben sandwich is created at Reuben's Restaurant in New York City. (This claim, however, is hotly disputed by Nebraska Cornhuskers who believe the sandwich was created in 1922 by grocer Reuben Kolakofsky during a poker game at the Blackstone Hotel in Omaha.)

1914: The outbreak of war in Europe leads to the expansion of U.S. pasta production. Until now, most macaroni and spaghetti come from Naples, Italy.

1915: Corning introduces Pyrex baking dishes.

1915: New York City's bagel baker union has almost 300 members.

1915: Per capita consumption of white sugar doubles from 1880 levels as Americans eat less molasses and brown sugar.

1916: The invention of the fortune cookie is attributed to George Jung, founder of the Hong Kong Noodle Co. in Los Angeles.

1916: Nathan Handwerker, a Polish shoemaker, opens a hot dog stand at Coney Island.

1916: War looms and the Edwardian good life becomes passé. Delmonico's, the most influential restaurant of the past century, closes.

1916: Piggly-Wiggly opens in Memphis, Tenn., and becomes the first supermarket chain.

1916: U.S. food prices jump 19 percent because of crop shortages, railcar shortages, and increased demand from war-strapped Britain. By 1917 price increases result in riots in Boston, New York, and Philadelphia.

1916: Streit's matzos are introduced in Manhattan.

1916: Cosmetics for women are frowned upon, unless the woman is of a certain age and so can perk up her faded looks with a bit of rouge. Most "cosmetics" are homemade—such as using lemon juice to lighten and soften hands, as promoted by the Sunkist cooperative. Quaker Oats promotes its product as "making flesh rather than fat, but enough fat for reserve force."

1917: The U.S. declares war on the Central Powers, joining an exhausted Britain and France, which have been fighting since 1914.

1917: Marshmallow Fluff is invented in Lynn, Mass.

1917: The hamburger becomes a "liberty sandwich" and sauerkraut is "liberty cabbage" during World War I.

1918: President Woodrow Wilson orders a 1,700-piece service of Lenox china, the first U.S.-made porcelain to be used in the White House.

1918: Canned tomato sauce is introduced. Canned mushrooms are introduced.

1919: Coca-Cola goes public. A $40 investment, with dividends reinvested, is worth $7.5 million in 1999.

1919: Hostess introduces its chocolate cupcakes, but the cakes are minus the vanilla filling and the icing fillip.

1919: John S. Campbell forms the Campbell Cereal Co. It has only one product—Malt-O-Meal, a malt-flavored, toasted hot cereal. In 1953 the company changes its name to the Malt-O-Meal Co. It's not until 1961 that the company makes a variation of its cornerstone cereal: Chocolate Malt-O-Meal.

1919: KitchenAid, seeking to move beyond supplying the U.S. Navy and commercial bakeries, produces a domestic version of its mixer. Four mixers roll off the Ohio assembly line each day and are sold by a female sales force that takes the sixty-five-pound product door to door. The model sells for $189.50.

1920–1929

THE ROARING TWENTIES began on a down note and ended in a funeral dirge. But in between, much of America had itself a grand old time.

Prohibitionists, busy in America since early in the 19th century, finally got their way in 1919 when the Volstead Act was ratified, making it illegal to produce, sell, or distribute alcoholic beverages.

Prohibition culminated in the unhappy coincidence of hard industrial conditions that drove many to drink heavily, a policy of saloons offering "free" lunches so that workers would ring up big liquor sales, and a turning against immigrants.

But much of Prohibition was window dressing. At the 1920 Democratic convention, delegates drank illegal whiskey catered free by San Francisco's mayor. Journalist and curmudgeon H.L. Mencken wrote, "Even in the most remote country districts, there is absolutely no place in which any man who desires to drink alcohol cannot get it."

And organized crime came into its own. Chicago bootlegger John Torrio made so much money from 1920 to 1924 that he retired to Italy in 1925 with a fortune of $30 million. Al Capone was Torrio's successor.

Restaurants, usually dependent on wine and liquor sales, closed by the droves. Many installed soda fountains to draw customers. And the speakeasy was born. These portable parties were epitomized by the operations of Mary Louise Cecilia "Texas" Guinan. Although often arrested for running speakeasies, Guinan gigged the police by wearing a gold police whistle around her neck and greeting her customers with the phrase "Hello, sucker."

Despite these disquieting developments on the crime front, the business of America's business was chugging along. In 1924 the number of cars produced by the four leading European carmakers equaled only eleven percent of the number of autos manufactured in America. The working class could drive, but the middle class was starting to fly. America was the economic power of the world, and its people were feeling their oats.

The Immigration Act of 1924 restricted immigration from Asia, Latin America, Africa, and eastern Europe, and Americans were into being Americans. Without an influx of new immigrants, the earlier arrivals were a captive audience for the "Americanization" of their diet. A program in southern California aimed

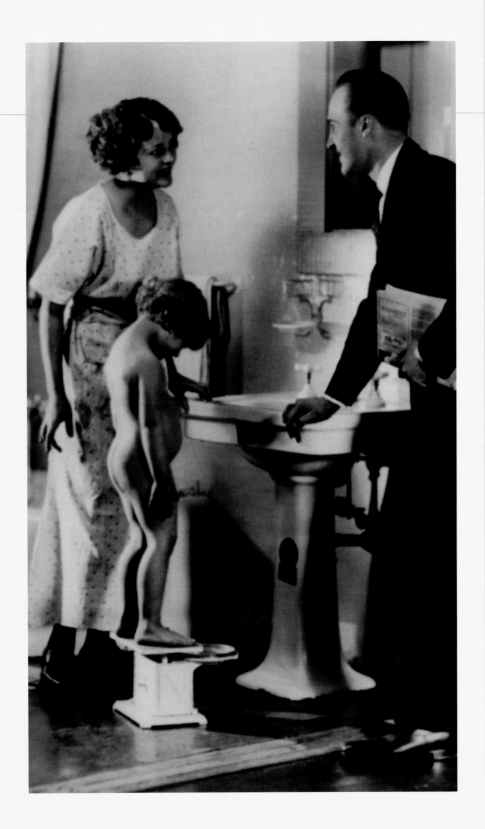

RIGHT: THE BEAUTY ETHIC HAS CHANGED, AND THE PLUMP IDEAL IS BEING REPLACED BY THE THINNER SILHOUETTE OF THE FLAPPERS.
Health O Meter, Inc.

KITCHEN MAID
STANDARD KITCHEN UNITS

Kitchen Maid Combination 1X

"Add-a-Unit" to your Kitchen Maid

Kitchen Maid Standard Units bring new opportunities to owners of the Kitchen Maid cabinet. You can add a cupboard of six shelves—set right against the Kitchen Maid, so it becomes a part of it. You can add a broom closet, to contain brooms, mops, and cleaning materials. You can put closet space all across the top, and have more convenience in your Kitchen Maid than you would find in a complete, old-fashioned pantry.

All units are finished with the same durable beauty as the original Kitchen Maid cabinet. Whether you now own a Kitchen Maid or not—investigate all the Kitchen Maid units. An ironing board which folds into the wall, the Pulmanook —a complete folding breakfast alcove, and many other units, all are described in our booklet of Kitchen Maid unit conveniences. You can install them in your present home or a new one. They cost less than building ordinary cupboards. Write today.

WASMUTH-ENDICOTT CO.
Andrews,   Indiana

The "Disappearing Ironing Board" folds into wall and takes no space when not in use. Can be installed in new or old homes.

The "Broom Closet" can be built in the wall, set in a corner, or grouped with the Kitchen Maid cabinet.

★ KITCHEN MAID
STANDARD UNIT SYSTEMS

"LET THE KITCHEN MAID BE YOUR KITCHEN AID"

ABOVE: KITCHENS CONTINUE TO BE PIECEMEAL AFFAIRS—NOTHING IS YET JOINED BY BUILT-IN CABINETS.

---

to teach Mexican-American girls to abandon their diet composed of vitamin-rich sauces made from tomatoes, chiles, nuts, and cheese in favor of white sauce—made from flour, butter, and milk—and hard sauce, a sugar-butter combination.

Nutrition confusion was on its way. Mary Pickford, Theda Bara, and Rudolph Valentino, the era's movie idols, promoted the idea of being thin. This, compounded by home economics classes in schools and the availability of women's magazines, started America on its ongoing war against fat.

The war behind them, American middle-class women were ready to cut their hair, step out into jobs, and have a good time. Problem was, the working classes were ready to do the same thing. So instead of the working classes taking the standard jobs of cleaning house and helping the missus with the children, jobs in factories and offices got the nod. Middle-class women then became dependent on their own cooking and housekeeping skills.

These women had big business ready to help. Between 1921 and 1929, the home appliance industry tripled its output. Americans spent $667 million on household appliances, a 500 percent increase over 1909 purchases.

Although kitchens remained at the rear of houses, it became common to locate the sink beneath a window so the person washing dishes (now more likely the homemaker than a paid employee) could enjoy a pleasant view.

Still obsessed with sanitation, enamel work surfaces began to replace zinc and wooden tops on the very popular Hoosier cabinets. Designers began introducing color into heretofore all-white (read clean) kitchens.

The kitchen was considered a workstation, and eating was almost always done in an adjoining breakfast room or dining room.

America was obsessed with progress, which meant prepared foods, particularly foods in cans. Although flavor may have suffered, Americans no longer had a winter diet of meat and bread and a summer diet of fruit and vegetables. Mostly, Americans were in high cotton.

But that was all about to change. October 1929 saw the stock market crash and a country that was faced with the worst economic trial of its history.

6 DRUMSTICKS

Nestle

WHEATIES IS INTRODUCED. The cereal is an accidental discovery by a Minneapolis health clinician and diet practitioner who, while mixing a batch of bran gruel for his patients, spills some on top of the hot stove. The quickly cooked spill is crisp and flaky, giving him the idea that perhaps bran could be made more palatable. His representative contacts the Washburn Crosby Co. (a forerunner of General Mills) to pitch the idea. Looking to diversify from flour, the company takes on the project.

Wheaties is credited with being the first product advertised with a singing radio commercial on—Christmas Eve 1926:

"Have you tried Wheaties?
"They're whole wheat with all of the bran.
"Won't you try Wheaties?
"For wheat is the best food of man."

In 1933 Wheaties introduces "Jack Armstrong, the All-American boy" to radio listeners. Played originally by Jim Ameche, "Jack" travels the world discovering adventure.

Good boy though he is, Jack endears himself to General Mills for the huge following he has among children. Jack Armstrong premiums send Wheaties sales off the charts. The first premium, in 1933, is an offer for a shooting plane in exchange for one box top and ten cents. The offer depletes Wheaties supplies around the country. Six months later the cereal is finally fully stocked in the nation's stores.

In 1939 Shirley Temple writes on her own letterhead to Jack Armstrong, for a hike-o-meter, enclosing a dime and a box top.

And then, of course, there is the famous Wheaties Breakfast of Champions boast. General Mills sponsors radio play-by-play of the Minneapolis Millers. The broadcast deal comes with a large billboard in the ballpark. A Minneapolis ad agency comes up with "Wheaties—The Breakfast of Champions." Every player who hits a home run that year, and for many years afterward, receives a case of Wheaties. Poor Joe Hauser hits sixty-nine for an American Association mark that year.

The sports endorsement deal is firmly established. Babe Ruth, Jack Dempsey, and Johnny Weismuller all testify to the benefits of Wheaties. Lou Gehrig and boxer Max Baer admit their love for Wheaties on radio programs sponsored by other cereal brands.

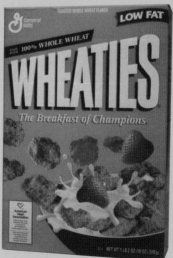

RIGHT: THE FIRST WHEATIES PACKAGING IS SHOWN FROM 1924 AND ITS ANNIVERSARY PACKAGING IN 1974. General Mills

Temptation!

Every lover of good candy is won over to **Baby Ruth.**

It is always welcome—always appreciated. A rare treat awaits you in its luscious opera cream center, dipped in delicious caramel, filled with crisply roasted-then-toasted peanuts, all coated with rich milk chocolate.

Better join the five-million-a-day who say it is America's Favorite Candy!

CURTISS CANDY COMPANY

New York   Boston   CHICAGO   San Francisco   Los Angeles

CURTISS **Baby Ruth** 5¢
America's Favorite 5¢

LEFT: CANDY IS DANDY WHEN CANDY BAR SALES SOAR AFTER WORLD WAR I. Nestle

ABOVE: A 1918 TOOTSIE ROLL AD
CELEBRATES THE RETURN OF
SOLDIERS FROM WORLD WAR I.
Tootise Roll Industries

RIGHT: TOOTSIE ROLLS WERE THE
FIRST PENNY CANDIES TO BE SOLD
INDIVIDUALLY WRAPPED.
Tootise Roll Industries

MEXICAN SALAD

[SERVES 4]

3 large green bell peppers

1 medium onion

4 medium ripe tomatoes

6 slices bacon

½ cup vinegar

½ teaspoon chili powder

CUT VEGETABLES in small chunks and mix. Cook bacon until crisp, break into pieces, stir in chili powder and vinegar over bacon and when it boils up, pour over vegetables. Serve on lettuce leaves.

— *The Woman's Club of Fort Worth Cook Book*
Compiled by Mrs. Clyde A. Lilly and Mrs. Olin Davis (1928)

"HE" SANDWICH

[YIELDS 3 SANDWICHES]

6 pieces hot buttered toast

6 crisp lettuce leaves

12 slices tomato

12 slices Bermuda onions

3 tablespoons chopped parsley

6 teaspoons mayonnaise

PLACE BETWEEN 2 pieces hot buttered toast one lettuce leaf; on top of this, 2 slices of tomato, 2 of onion and ½ teaspoon parsley. Cover with 1 teaspoon mayonnaise. A little extra salt may be added because tomatoes always absorb more salt than any other vegetable.

— *The Woman's Club of Fort Worth Cook Book*

RADIO NEWS

The Jolly Happy Wonder Bakers and their peppy orchestra in the WEAF broadcasting studio, New York. Gathered around the microphone you see the Wonder Bakers clad in uniforms of spotless white.

The Happy Wonder Bakers broadcast over the great NBC Red Network beginning on Tuesday, January 21. Tune in on this delightful program of songs, music and special features.

WONDER BREAD
IT'S SLO-BAKED

Baked by the Bakers of Hostess Cake and Wonder Pan Rolls

WONDER BREAD IS INTRODUCED IN 1920. IT WILL BECOME ONE OF THE FIRST NATIONALLY KNOWN BREAD BRANDS AND BE CONSIDERED THE EPITOME OF MODERN CONVENIENCE. NO MORE TEDIOUS BAKING, NOR, AFTER 1927, ANY SLICING REQUIRED.

Interstate Bakeries Corporation

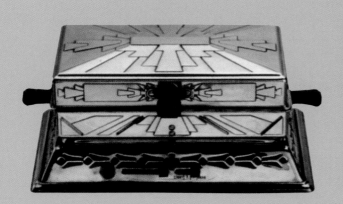

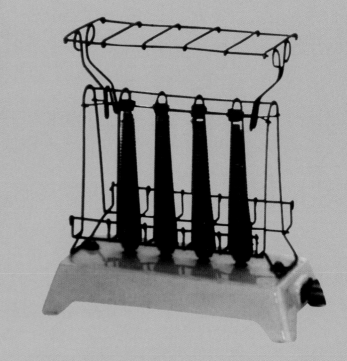

America's love affair with technology was in full bloom in the 1920s. Flush with money, these geegaws were just the ticket to feeling modern.

With the advent of homes outfitted with electricity, the power companies solicited inventions—they wanted consumers to use the power. Toasters, a relatively simple appliance, were one of the first appliances to go middle class. Designs were Deco, then Moderne, then fat and sleek in the 1950s, after a patriotic pause during the 1940s so the vital metal could be used for the war effort.

There were follies along the way, too, like the Multitoaster which was a skyscraper of an appliance that could perform all the breakfast functions one might need under one roof and on one plug.

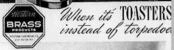

RIGHT: THE SMALL KTICHEN APPLIANCE INDUSTRY
BOOMED FOLLOWING WORLD WAR I. AS MORE AND
MORE AMERICAN HOMES BECAME WIRED FOR
ELECTRICITY, THE POWER PROVIDERS ENCOURAGED
COMPANIES TO COME UP WITH MORE USES FOR THE
NEW CONVENIENCE. BREAKFAST APPLIANCES WERE
ESPECIALLY POPULAR BECAUSE ELECTRICITY USE
WAS MINIMAL IN THE MORNING—MOST CONSUMERS
USED IT FOR NIGHTTIME ILLUMINATION. TOASTED
BREAD HAD NEVER BEEN CONSIDERED A BREAKFAST
FOOD UNTIL THE TOASTER MANUFACTURERS BEGAN
ADVERTISING WITH THE SUGGESTION TO "MAKE
TOAST YOUR BREAKFAST."

The Schenectady Museum

CHICKEN PUDDING

[Serves 6–8]

2 chickens, cut into serving pieces

salt and pepper

8 eggs

1 quart milk

3 tablespoons melted butter

1 teaspoon salt

2 heaping teaspoons baking powder

Sifted all-purpose flour

GRAVY

Broth from cooking chicken

1 tablespoon flour

⅓ cup melted butter

PLACE CHICKENS in pot with just enough water to cover. When boiled quite tender, season with salt and pepper; let them simmer 10 to 15 minutes longer. Take chicken from broth and remove all bones, reserving broth. Place meat in well-buttered pudding dish, season again, if necessary, adding a few bits of butter.

Beat eggs until light. Add the milk, butter, salt and baking powder. Add enough sifted flour to make a batter like pancakes. Pour over chicken.

Bake 1 hour in 350-degree oven.

Make a gravy of the broth that remained from the cooking of the chicken, adding the flour stirred into the butter; let it boil up, putting in more water if necessary.

Serve hot in a gravy boat with the pudding.

— *The White House Cook Book* by Hugo Ziemann and Mrs. F. L. Gillette
(Saalfield Publishing, 1924)

Canning in the 1920s is still very much a local affair, with canneries around the country putting up their own products. These labels show the diversity in the country, including squid canned in California with bilingual labels for Italian-American customers.

ABOVE: ONE THING AMERICANS HAVE ALWAYS BEEN ABLE TO DO IS SELL. JOE LONG WAS A PRIME EXAMPLE. DURING ONE LONG DUSTY WEEK IN THE TEXAS PANHANDLE IN 1929, HE SOLD EIGHT WASHING MACHINES. THAT'S JOE ON HORSEBACK; THE ASSEMBLAGE ON THE LEFT IS THE "JACKASS EXPRESS." Maytag

ABOVE: AMERICA STILL THINKS NOTHING OF RACIAL STEREOTYPES.

ABOVE: THE GREEN GIANT DIDN'T LOOK QUITE SO JOLLY IN HIS 1928 INCARNATION. Pillsbury

Westinghouse
ELECTRIC UTILITIES FOR THE HOUSEHOLD

WESTINGHOUSE ELECTRIC

KITCHENS CONTINUE TO
BE PIECEMEAL AFFAIRS—
NOTHING IS YET JOINED
BY BUILT-IN CABINETS.

In the Modern Kitchen

Because of their cleanly, beautiful silver-like appearance, "Wear-Ever" utensils are preferred by women who wish their kitchens to be as modern and attractive as the other rooms of the home.

"Wear-Ever"
Aluminum Cooking Utensils

are made from hard, thick sheet aluminum, without joints or seams in which particles of food can lodge. Cannot chip or peel—are pure and safe.

Replace utensils that wear out with utensils that "Wear-Ever"

Look for the "Wear-Ever" trade mark on the bottom of each utensil

The Aluminum Cooking Utensil Co.
Department 10   New Kensington, Pa.

In Canada, "Wear-Ever" utensils are made by Northern Aluminum Company, Ltd., Toronto, Ont.

STRIPED PARFAIT

[SERVES 6]

1 cup powdered sugar

¼ cup water

1 egg white beaten

2 teaspoons vanilla

Pinch of salt

2 cups heavy cream, stiffly beaten

Food coloring of choice

2 ounces baking chocolate, melted

BOIL SUGAR and water together gently until it spins a thread. Add this very slowly to the beaten egg white, beating constantly until thick. Add vanilla and salt and combine with the cream.

Leave one portion of the mixture white. To a second portion, add food coloring to make any color desired. To a third portion, add melted chocolate. These may be frozen in small pans slipped into the Frigidaire freezing compartment, or may all be frozen in one tray, separated by oiled paper. Any combination of colors may be placed in layers in a parfait glass. This is an excellent way to carry out a color scheme for a party.

— Adapted from Frigidaire's *Frozen Delights* (1927)

ABOVE: THE ENCLOSED REFRIGERATOR "MONITOR" IN 1927 REVOLUTIONIZED HOME-FRONT REFRIGERATION. THE MESS AND BOTHER OF MELTING ICE WERE NO LONGER A NECESSARY BYPRODUCT OF KEEPING FOOD COLD. General Electric

PINEAPPLE
UPSIDE DOWN CAKE

[SERVES 8]

1 pound, 4 ounce can sliced pineapple

¼ cup butter

⅔ cup brown sugar, firmly packed

Maraschino cherries

1½ cups all-purpose flour

¾ cup sugar

1½ teaspoons baking powder

½ teaspoon salt

½ cup whole milk

¼ cup shortening

1 egg

1 teaspoon lemon juice

1 teaspoon vanilla

¼ teaspoon grated lemon peel

DRAIN PINEAPPLE, reserving 2 tablespoons syrup.

Melt butter in 10-inch cast iron skillet. Stir in brown sugar until blended. Remove from heat.

Arrange pineapple slices in sugar mixture. Place a maraschino cherry in center of each pineapple slice.

Combine flour, sugar, baking powder, and salt. Add milk and shortening; beat 2 minutes. Add egg, reserved syrup, lemon juice, vanilla, and lemon peel. Beat 2 minutes.

Pour over pineapple in skillet, spreading evenly. Bake in 350-degree oven for 40 minutes. Cool on wire rack for 5 minutes. Invert onto serving plate. Serve warm.

— Dole Pineapple

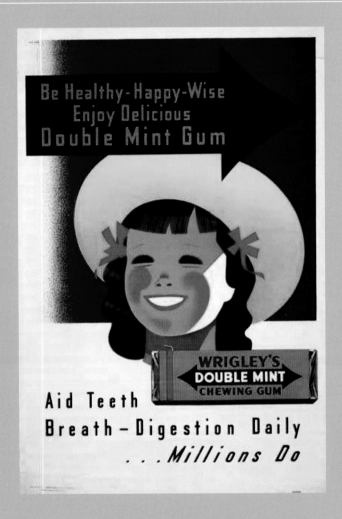

WRIGLEY'S CHEWING GUM
EMPLOYS MASTER ARTISTS
TO DESIGN ADVERTISING
BILLBOARDS AND POSTERS,
THE MAIN ADVERTISING
VENUES. Library of Congress

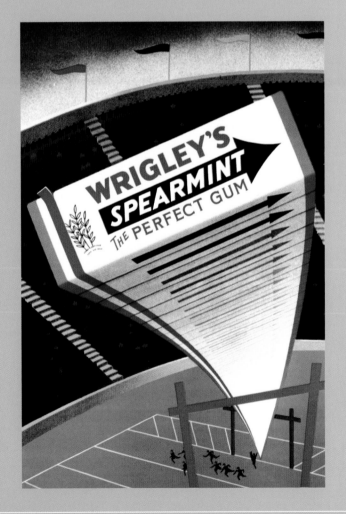

1920: In January Prohibition goes into effect. Although drinking will continue and will lead to the establishment of speakeasies, Prohibition leads to an increase in sales of coffee, soft drinks, and ice cream sodas. Many bars convert to soda fountains or tearooms to stay in business.

1920: Italian immigrants in California begin growing and popularizing broccoli. Since Thomas Jefferson's time, it has been a vegetable for the rich.

1920: The 19th Amendment, giving women the right to vote, is ratified.

1920: From now until 1935, sales of lettuce triple—most of it the iceberg variety. This variety is a boon to growers and suppliers, who find they can ship the dense heads nationwide with little or no damage to the lettuce.

1920: Wonder Bread is introduced.

1920: La Choy Food Products gets its start in Detroit. [A grocer and a Korean he has known since both attended the University of Michigan team up to sell bean sprouts in jars.] In 1922, they begin canning the sprouts.

1921: The first White Castle hamburger stand opens in Wichita, Kan. The white of the stones suggests cleanliness; the castle façade suggests stability. The little burgers cost 5 cents apiece and are marketed with the slogan "Buy 'em by the sack." Paper napkins come on the market in 1925, and White Castle locations follow by developing folding paper hats that can be changed often. "Program-mic" hot dog-shape kiosks and cone shape stands architecture becomes the rage in restaurants.

1921: Kandy Kake, a chocolate-covered caramel and peanut bar, is introduced. Later it is renamed Baby Ruth after President Grover Cleveland's daughter, one of the few babies born in the White House and an object of much public affection.

1921: The American Birth Control League (later Planned Parenthood) is founded by Margaret Sanger and Maryware Dennett.

1921: McCormick & Co. now has a nine-story building where it produces more than 800 products under its various brand names. The company's cafeteria offers hot lunches for 15 cents to 25 cents.

1921: Table-salt makers iodize salt with potassium iodide to prevent goiter, an enlarged thyroid, but the process is not mandatory.

1921: The Eskimo Pie, first named I-Scream, is introduced.

1921: Quaker Oats introduces quick-cooking oatmeal.

1921: Betty Crocker is born.

The Washburn Crosby Co. comes up with the idea for Betty after running a promotion for a pincushion shaped like a flour sack. The company thinks it would be nice to have a "personal" response to consumer inquiries.

Crocker is used as the surname to honor a retired director of the company, William G. Crocker. Betty, it is felt, is a friendly name. Women employees submit sample Betty Crocker signatures, and the most distinctive is chosen to be Betty's own.

Until 1936 Betty is faceless. She is played by different women on various editions of the "Betty Crocker Cooking School of the Air," daytime radio's first cooking show. Letters and advice are dispensed by a staff of home economists in the company's Home Service Department, which is later to become the Betty Crocker Kitchen.

1921: Sanka Decaffeinated Coffee is introduced.

1922: Two Canadians isolate the hormone from canine pancreatic juices to save the life of a child dying of diabetes. This discovery will lead to commercial insulin—the first treatment for diabetes other than diet limitations.

1922: *Fruit, Garden and Home* debuts. It will become a star as *Better Homes & Gardens*.

1923: The May issue of *Women's Home Companion* publishes an article that includes the lines, "With the revolution in clothes has come a revolution in our attitude toward avoirdupois. Once weight was an asset: Now it's a liability, both physical and esthetic."

1923: Henry Ford manufactures charcoal briquettes to recycle sawdust from his car factories.

1924: Tijuana, Mexico restaurant owner (and Italian immigrant) Caesar Cardini comes up with the showy, tableside-prepared Caesar salad. Later, the International Society of Epicures in Paris votes the dish "the greatest recipe to originate from the Americas in 50 years."

1924: The Popsicle is patented.

1925: Honey Maid Graham Crackers is introduced. By the end of the century, Americans eat more than 2.2 billion Honey Maids a year.

1925: The average American homemaker prepares all her food at home. By 1965 seventy-five percent to ninety percent of the food she uses has undergone some sort of factory processing.

1925: Canned tomato juice introduced and is an instant hit.

1925: Howard Johnson opens a restaurant in Wollaston, Mass.

1925: General Electric introduces the first hermetically sealed domestic refrigerator.

1925: The Minnesota Canning Co., around since 1903, is known for its canned kernel corn. But, like most things American, the company wants to grow. A company official returns from a European trip with a new variety of green pea. It isn't a pretty pea—it is wrinkled, oblong, and quite large. But what the pea lacks in beauty, it makes up in sweet flavor and tenderness. The company's customers don't bite, however, and ignore the big ugly duckling.

The company won't abandon its orphan child. Instead, they decide to bring the peas to the forefront and name them the "Green Giants." In 1950 Minnesota Valley Canning Co. becomes the Green Giant Co.

1926: Milk Duds are introduced.

1926: To use up leftovers, the Cobb salad—a chopped salad made with avocado, lettuce, celery, tomato, bacon, chicken, chives, hard-boiled egg, watercress, and Roquefort cheese, is created at the Brown Derby in Los Angeles by owner Bob Cobb. The Brown Derby is one example of restaurant "programmic architecture" (the building looks like a derby) springing up along the nation's roads.

1926: The Russian Tea Room in New York City is opened by members of the Russian Imperial Ballet. It becomes a meeting place for Russian artists, writers, and musicians as well as for America's show-business crowd.

1926: Hormel introduces canned ham.

1926: In Connecticut, Polish immigrant Harry Lender begins making bagels.

1927: General Electric introduces the first direct-drive dishwasher with revolutionary systems that are still in use at the turn of the twenty-first century.

1927: Pez is introduced in Austria as a peppermint breath mint for smokers. In 1948, the plastic dispensers are introduced and the United States begins to manufacture the brand and market it to children.

1927: Milk is homogenized.

1927: General Electric introduces the revolutionary monitor-top refrigerator. The motor is sealed in a case that perches on top of the appliance, and it requires no maintenance. As production picks up, the price falls from $600 for the clunky 1920 model to an average of $90 by 1940. But until after World War II, many people use iceboxes, which have to be regularly reloaded with ice and the trays of water underneath discarded. Even $90 is a lot of money. "No more worry while away," an early ad states. "The cost of spoiled and wasted foods no longer interferes—electric refrigeration keeps them fresh and pure for days. Go away when you like—return to find the most delicate foods in perfect condition."

Kraft

1927: Stainless steel cutlery debuts.

1927: Kool-Aid is introduced in powdered form. Hastings, Neb., chemist Edwin Perkins has developed a fruit syrup in six flavors for consumers. It is marketed under the name Fruit Smack and goes on the market in 1920. But inspired by the suc-cess of Jell-O gelatin, he concentrates Fruit Smack into powder and packages them in envelopes. He changes the name to Kool-Ade, which becomes Kool-Aid.

1927: The automatic toaster debuts.

1927: Cut-Rite Wax Paper is introduced.

1928: Sliced bread is introduced.

1928: Drumsticks, a frozen ice cream cone, is introduced.

1928: Reeses Peanut Butter Cups debuts. Named for the man who created them, they are a peanut butter-chocolate combination still among the most popular candy bars today.

1928: The Bureau of Prohibition reports that nearly 70,000 doctors are using alcohol prescription books. Doctors could prescribe ½ pint per patient every ten days, but they couldn't use more than one hundred prescriptions (one book) every ninety days.

1928: Broccoli is new to the United States and leads to the New Yorker cartoon by Carl Rose (with a caption by E. B. White) that has a young child saying, "I say it's spinach, and I say to hell with it."

1928: Butterfinger Candy Bars are introduced.

1928: Peter Pan Peanut Butter is introduced.

1928: Rice Krispies are introduced.

1928: Velveeta Process Cheese Spread is introduced. It's promoted as a product that children will like.

1929: Clarence Birdseye masters the quick-freezing of vegetables. In the 1930s, his patents allow many kinds of fresh foods to be sold from low-temperature cases.

1929: The ruby red variety of grapefruit is discovered as a mutation on a McAllen, Texas, farm.

1929: Nestle purchases Peter's Chocolate, a European company specializing in chocolate for chefs and bakers. Peter's Chocolate developed the world's first milk chocolate, using Henri Nestle's condensed milk.

Kraft

Nestle's first claim to fame was to develop the first infant food in 1867 in Switzerland.

1929: Oscar Mayer Wieners are packed with yellow bands for brand identification.

1929: 7-Up enters the beverage market.

1929: Gerber introduces canned baby food.

1929: The stock market crashes.

ABOVE: TEXAS RED GRAPEFRUIT (SO CALLED BECAUSE THEY HANG IN CLUSTERS ON THE TREE MUCH LIKE GRAPES) ARE "DISCOVERED" IN 1929, A BUD MUTATION ON A PINK GRAPEFRUIT TREE. Texas Sweet

L IKE MANY AMERICAN decades, the 1930s were a dichotomy of despair and progress.

The U.S. stock market crashed in October 1929. As the next decade opened, America imposed the Smoot-Hawley tariff, which raised import taxes on goods from abroad. Our depression became the world's depression.

In New York City, the International Apple Shippers Association gave its fruit on credit to jobless men to sell on street corners and to help the association dispose of its surplus. By November 1930, 6,000 men were selling apples on New York sidewalks. By the spring of 1931, the city declared the men a nuisance and ordered them off the street.

A combination of record wheat yields that drove down prices followed by a devastating drought hit American farmers with a one-two punch. In 1931 some Kansas counties waived taxes to help farmers. Banks began to foreclose on loans, forcing farmers off the land.

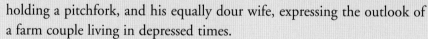
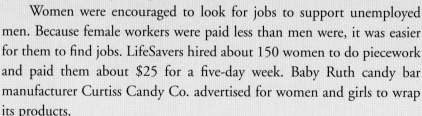

Grant Wood painted *American Gothic*, a composition of a dour man in overalls holding a pitchfork, and his equally dour wife, expressing the outlook of a farm couple living in depressed times.

Women were encouraged to look for jobs to support unemployed men. Because female workers were paid less than men were, it was easier for them to find jobs. LifeSavers hired about 150 women to do piecework and paid them about $25 for a five-day week. Baby Ruth candy bar manufacturer Curtiss Candy Co. advertised for women and girls to wrap its products.

In 1934, "Okies" and "Arkies," devastated by the weather in the Dust Bowl, begin migrating to California. More than 350,000 farmers moved west over the next five years.

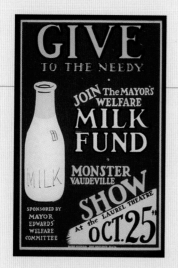

Yet time also brought progress. In 1930 Auguste Escoffier, creator of the Peach Melba dessert and father of modern cuisine, presided over a dinner to celebrate the opening of the Hotel Pierre on New York's Fifth Avenue. In 1935, Pan Am Clipper flights provided the first hot meals served in the air.

Production of home appliances escalated; America was enchanted with modernism. Design became streamlined, function following form.

The Detroit London Chop House opened in 1939 with 75-cent steak dinners and 25-cent Scotch-and-sodas. The Pump Room opened in Chicago the same year. Lawry's The Prime Rib premiered in Los Angeles (later to pioneer valet parking).

Women's clubs came into their own as ladies of leisure banded together through charitable events, gardening, and bridge. Light club food (creamy, dainty, and sweet) was the norm. The absence of liquor and domestic help, to say nothing of the gloomy economy, made most entertaining more a family event.

Americans found solace in simple things. Marshmallows were a craze, as were candy and silly garnishes like pineapple circles and maraschino cherries. Waffles were the rage, much simpler to make now that electric waffle irons were available. Waffles were served for breakfast or lunch, and for Sunday night suppers.

Americans were circling the hearth as a foreign war loomed.

OPPOSITE AND ABOVE: DOROTHEA LANGE'S PHOTOGRAPHS OF THIS
MIGRANT WOMAN AND HER CHILDREN BECOME THE SYMBOL OF THE
MISERIES AND DISPLACEMENTS OF THE 1930S. Library of Congress

FRENCH DRESSING

[YIELDS ³⁄₄ CUP]

2 tablespoons cold water

½ teaspoon unflavored gelatin

2 tablespoons vinegar

1 teaspoon onion juice (extracted by grating onion)

1 teaspoon salt

Pepper

8 drops Worcestershire sauce

½ cup olive oil

POUR COLD water in bowl and sprinkle gelatin on top of water; add vinegar. Place bowl over boiling water and stir until gelatin is dissolved. Add seasonings and cool (but don't allow it to thicken). Pour into bottle, add oil, and shake until well-blended. Use other seasonings as desired.

This dressing will remain in emulsion, but don't place it in the refrigerator or it will acquire a jelly-like consistency.

— *Knox Gelatin Desserts, Salads, Candies and Frozen Dishes* (1933)

ABOVE: SURE-JELL, A POWDERED PECTIN THAT ENSURES THE SETTING OF HOME-CANNED JAMS AND JELLIES, APPEARS NATIONALLY IN 1935. Kraft

It's a product that spawns millions of jokes, but Spam has been a hit ever since it was introduced to the market in the 1930s. Especially in Hawaii, which has to import so much of its food supply, the "miracle meat" is a staple. Soldiers, too, eat their share of Spam, and at least one generation of children grow up eating Spam sandwiches. Hormel

February, 1931   LADIES' HOME JOURNAL.

HOT OFF THE GRIDDLE

.....and new as tomorrow

BANANA WAFFLES

are

SOMETHING TO *Rave* **ABOUT**

General Mills

ABOVE AND RIGHT:
GREAT MINDS THINK
ALIKE. IN 1930
FAMILY-OWNED JIFFY
INTRODUCES ITS
BAKING MIX. IN 1931
GENERAL MILLS
FOLLOWS WITH
BISQUICK.

Jiffy Co.

Edwin Perkins, owner of Perkins
Products Co. in Hastings, Neb., decides
to fiddle with his most popular item,
a soft drink syrup called Fruit Smack.
He concentrates the syrup into a
powder and packages it in envelopes.
He changes the name to Kool-Ade
(as it appears in this 1934 ad) and
later changes it to Kool-Aid, as it
appears on these later packages. Kraft

CHICKEN SALAD

[SERVES 2-3]

2 cups diced chicken

½ cup stuffed olives, plus more for garnish

1 cup celery, optional

½ cup mayonnaise

½ teaspoon salt

⅔ cup lettuce broken in small parts

PLACE CHICKEN, olives, and celery in mixing bowl, add mayonnaise and salt, and mix well with a fork. Serve on crisp lettuce from the "Frigidaire Hydrator," or crisp endive can be used; garnish the salad with several stuffed olives.

— *Frigidaire Recipe Book* (1932)

SHRIMP LOUISIANE

[SERVES 4]

1 teaspoon onion, minced

4 tablespoons butter

2 cups peeled shrimp, fresh or canned, broken in pieces

4 tablespoons flour

1 teaspoon salt

1 teaspoon chili powder

2 cups milk

4 tablespoons ketchup

2 tablespoons parsley, minced

SAUTÉ ONION in butter until soft; add shrimp and brown. Stir in flour, salt, chili powder and then, gradually, the milk. Cook 5 minutes. Add ketchup and parsley. Steam several minutes. Serve over hot rice.

— Gebhardt's *Mexican Cookery for American Homes* (1932)

In 1933, Ruth Wakefield, innkeeper of the Toll House in Whitman, Mass., takes a shortcut when making cookies. Instead of melting semisweet chocolate to add to the batter, she breaks up a chocolate bar and drops the pieces into the batter. And so, America's beloved chocolate chip cookie is born.

The recipe soon finds its way into print in a local newspaper and becomes quite the local rage.

In an unusual juxtapostion, Nestle began manufacturing its chocolate morsels in response to a popular cookie recipe. Eventually, the company buys the rights to the Toll House name. Nestle

Drink **Coca-Cola** Delicious and Refreshing

Thru 50 years...1886 to 1936
The pause that refreshes

Fashions in clothes change. But human thirst is always the same. Since the first ice-cold Coca-Cola made a *pause refreshing* in 1886, its fame has spread . . . from city to city . . . country to country . . . around the world . . . welcome everywhere, because ice-cold Coca-Cola is what refreshment ought to be . . . pure . . . wholesome . . . delicious.

ICE-COLD EVERY DAY IN THE YEAR

5¢

7up LITHIATED **LEMON SODA**

Seven-Up Settles the Stomach
For Hospital or home use.

The added citrate neutralize free acid. The sugar is inverted . . . burns clean 7-Up is more than a mixer . . It blends out the harsh features. Dispels hangovers. Takes the "ouch" out of grouch.

Slenderizing

PRINTED IN U.S.A.

SANITARY BRAND **Root Beer** ARTIFICIAL COLOR
SANITARY BOTTLING WORKS
3824 DEODAR STREET
INDIANA HARBOR, INDIANA
TELEPHONE INDIANA HARBOR 1627

CONTENTS 24 FLUID OUNCES

LEFT: OSCAR MAYER WAS ALWAYS AN INNOVATOR. IN 1924, THE COMPANY BEGAN OFFERING ITS BACON SLICED AND WRAPPED— TWO CONVENIENCES THAT SAVED THE CONSUMER TIME AT THE MEAT COUNTER. IN 1929, THE COMPANY BEGAN PACKAGING ITS HOTDOGS WITH YELLOW BANDS TO DISTINGUISH THEM FROM OTHER BRANDS. IN 1936, ON THE SOFTER SIDE OF BUSINESS, THE WEINERMOBILE BEGAN ITS LIFE AS A TRAVELING AMBASSADOR FOR FRANKFURTER FUN.
Kraft

Kraft

ABOVE: SWANKYSWIGS, CHEESE SPREADS PACKAGED IN REUSABLE GLASSES, ARE INTRODUCED IN 1933. BY THE END OF THE CENTURY THIS GLASSWARE IS HIGHLY COLLECTIBLE. Kraft

LEFT: In 1936 Homer Laughlin introduces colorful Fiesta ware, which would prove to be one of the most enduring patterns for American tables. After a 14-year break beginning in 1972, the company reintroduces Fiesta, in new colors, in the 1980s.

ABOVE: Chili powder, the all-American combination of the Southwest, is already a presence in 1930.

LEFT: Candy is going big time in 1931—it's an affordable indulgence during a very rough decade.

Tootsie Roll Industries

CRIMSON CRYSTAL DESSERT

[Serves 6]

4-serving size strawberry gelatin

1 ½ cups boiling water

¼ cup maraschino cherry juice

Juice of 1 lemon

12 maraschino cherries, quartered

Dissolve gelatin in boiling water. Add fruit juices. Turn into 10-by-5-inch pan. Chill until firm. Cut into cubes. Pile into sherbet glasses with cherries.

—*Quick, Easy Jell-O Wonder Dishes* (1930)

Maytag

Frigidaire

ABOVE: THE TEXAS RANGERETTES INSPECT THE GE
"TALKING" KITCHEN AT THE TEXAS CENTENNIAL
EXPOSITION, 1936. Schenectady Museum

ABOVE AND OPPOSITE: DESPITE THE HARD ECONOMIC TIMES OF THE 1930S, THE DESIGN AND DEMAND FOR TIMESAVING HOME APPLIANCES CONTINUE TO GROW. THE REFRIGERATOR IS A 1939 MODEL. MAYTAG PROMOTES ITS WASHERS IN SEVERAL FILMS, INCLUDING *BLONDIE MEETS THE BOSS*. BUT THE COMPANY DOESN'T NEED TO PROMOTE ITS WASHERS TO HARD-WORKING FARM FAMILIES, WHO KNOW A HELPING HAND WHEN THEY SEE ONE. Maytag

SAUSAGE-STUFFED BAKED APPLES

[SERVES 4]

4 apples
1 pound pork sausage
1 cup sugar
1 tablespoon butter
1 cup water

PEEL APPLES and core. Stuff with sausage. Place in baking dish. Sprinkle with sugar and dot with butter. Add water, cover, and bake in 350-degree oven.

— *Tempting Meat Recipes 1935* by the National Live Stock and Meat Board

ABOVE: IN THE 1930S, HONEY MAID GRAHAM CRACKERS PLAY TO THE YOUNGER AUDIENCE. THE LEAPFROGGING BOY APPEARS ON A 1939 BILLBOARD. CHILDREN RUNNING HOME FROM SCHOOL APPEAR IN A 1939 MAGAZINE ADVERTISEMENT. Nabisco

1930–1939 Timeline

1930: The average household works 91 days to buy a year's worth of food and spends 25 percent of the household income on food.

1930: More than 4 million people are unemployed; the number rises to 8 million in 1931 and 12 million in 1932 (a total of 25 percent of the workforce).

1930: The Brenham Creamery Co. in Texas changes its name to Blue Bell Creameries Inc. The company has been making ice cream since 1911 in a wooden tub filled with ice, and has a production ceiling of two gallons a day. In 1936 the company buys its first refrigerated truck and continuous freezer. In 1939 1-pint ice cream containers are used for the first time.

1930: The average distance between the fields where fruits and vegetables are grown and the markets in which they are sold is 1,500 miles.

1930: Birdseye introduces frozen food; electric stoves appear.

1930: Pat and Harry Olivieri of Pat's Restaurant in Philadelphia claim to have created the Philadelphia cheese-steak, although they say the cheese won't be added until 1948.

1930: Twinkies are invented by a Hostess plant manager.

1930: Baking mix, a biscuit combination that needs only to have liquid added, is the brainchild of Mabel White Holmes. Holmes and her husband own the Chelsea Milling Co. in Chelsea, Mich., so they have the means to put their idea to the test.

In 1930 they introduce Jiffy Baking Mix. Later, they add pie crust mix, cake mixes, and corn muffin mixes to their line.

1931: St. Louis widow Irma Rombauer publishes *The Joy of Cooking*.

1931: General Mills executive Carl Smith, so the company lore goes, borrows a brilliant idea after a 1930 train trip. While traveling from Portland to San Francisco, Smith orders biscuits with his meal in the dining car.

Because it is past the dinner hour, he is surprised to quickly get fresh, hot biscuits. He discovers that the ingredients for the biscuits had been combined much earlier.

The chef on the Southern Pacific obviously has a great mind.

Back home, Smith presents the idea to the General Mills chemist. The problem is finding a way to keep shortening fresh and a leavening agent powerful.

By 1931 Bisquick is on the market, with the claim that the baking mix "Makes Anybody a Perfect Biscuit Maker."

1931: Built-in sinks begin to replace freestanding models.

1931: The Tootsie Pop, a hard candy shell with a chewy chocolate center on a stick, is invented.

1932: Maytag advertises its washers as a boon for the hard-working family.

1932: San Antonio candy-maker C. Elmer Doolin stops in a cafe for a sandwich and is served a side dish of corn chips. He pays the cafe owner $100 for his converted potato ricer and the recipe for "tortillas fritas." Fritos are born, as Doolin and his family begin producing 10 pounds per day. They eventually move their operation to Dallas.

1932: *Better Homes and Gardens* publishes its first diet article.

1932: Hotpoint introduces the single-slice toaster.

1932: Sales of Ford automobiles to farmers fall to 55,000, down from 650,000 in 1929.

1932: *Family Circle*, the first check out magazine to be sold in supermarkets, debuts as an entertainment-oriented publication.

1932: The bagel is first mentioned in American print. The first bagels sold in a supermarket were from Lender's Bagel Bakery in New Haven, Conn., in 1955. It was also the first to sell frozen bagels, in 1962.

1933: Prohibition is repealed when Utah becomes the 36th state to ratify the 21st Amendment.

1933: The E. and J. Gallo winery is founded in Modesto, Calif., by Ernest Gallo, 24, and his brother Julio, 23. The brothers sink $5,900 into the operation, which will become the largest U.S. winemaker.

1933: Canned pineapple juice is first introduced, at the Chicago World's Fair. It would seem a simple thing, but Dole has been trying to produce pineapple juice since as early as 1910, but it had no process to glean the juice from the pineapple. Without breaking the cells of the pineapple, the aroma and the flavor are poor. Finally, two company engineers come up with a process that works. Not only will the compa-

ny sell juice to consumers, but other by-products such as liquid sugar, ascorbic acid, citric acid, and cattle feed can be made from the rinds.

1934: Refrigerators become modern as the exterior compressor (the monitor top) is placed inside the cabinet.

1934: Ritz Crackers are introduced.

1934: Hard times lead to making do. Restaurants crop up in unlikely locations, like tents and trailers.

1934: Campbell's begins selling Chicken Noodle and Cream of Mushroom Soups.

1934: McCormick & Co. introduces the "finger mold" extract bottle for safety's sake. Tins of the company's ground spices are outfitted with spoon-sift tops.

1934: Prohibition repeal takes effect.

1935: Pan Am serves the first hot in-flight meals.

1935: General Electric introduces the first food waste disposer—it's named the Disposall.

1935: A Connecticut woman comes up with an additive-free whole grain bread for her asthmatic son. The brand becomes Pepperidge Farm.

1935: The Social Security Act is signed into law.

1936: Howard Johnson's first restaurant opens, on Cape Cod. During the next couple of decades, the restaurants begin appearing along New England highways and spread throughout the country.

1936: Stuckey's gets its start when William and Ethel Stuckey open a roadside stand in Georgia to sell pecans to motorists en route to and from Florida.

1936: American Airlines begins serving meals on its DC3s.

1936: The first commercially baked Girl Scout cookies are marketed for 25 cents a box. The only flavor is

Dole

shortbread. The first cookies had been baked and sold by Girl Scout Troop 127 in Philadelphia to raise money for summer camp.

1936: Native American migrant farmworker Florence Owens Thompson becomes a symbol of the depression in Dorothea Lange's photograph.

1936: Duncan Hines' *Adventures in Good Eating* is published. He becomes the country's roving dining critic.

1937: Sylvan Goldman, owner of the Standard Food Markets and Humpty Dumpty Stores in Oklahoma City, devises a shopping cart by fabricating lawn chairs into a frame that holds two hand baskets. He figures if the shoppers can carry more, they'll buy more. But the first shopping cart is a hard sell. Men find the carts less than masculine and women don't see the point—they're accustomed to shopping often. Finally, Goldman pays "shoppers" to cruise the stores using the carts.

1937: Spam is introduced.

1937: The Waring Blendor is introduced as a bartender's tool. Although band leader Fred Waring lends his name and finances the appliance's development, the machine is invented by Fred Osius, one of the founders of the Hamilton Beach Co.

1937: Refrigerators are in more than 2 million U.S. households.

1937: Kraft rolls out Kraft Dinner—a boxed meal that sells for 19 cents with an advertising slogan of "A Meal for Four in Nine Minutes." At the end of the century, 1 million boxes a day of Kraft Macaroni & Cheese are sold in the United States. In 1998, the company brings out a microwave version.

1937: *Fortune* magazine reports that hired domestics work in 70 percent of upper-income homes, 42 per-

Kraft

cent of upper middle-class homes, 14 percent of lower middle-class homes, and 6 percent of poor homes.

1938: Teflon is accidentally created by a DuPont chemist who wants to develop a refrigerant. Eventually, Teflon coats 75 percent of the pots and pans sold in the United States.

1938: Copper-bottom Revere Ware debuts.

1938: Herman W. Lay introduces the potato chip for the masses. Lay's Potato Chips will become the best-selling potato chip in the country.

1939: Nestle Tollhouse Morsels are introduced.

1939: Despite the depression, America continues to believe in technology. Electric mixers, vacuum cleaners, and irons are manufactured with modern, streamlined designs.

1939: Only 3 percent of Americans have enough income to pay taxes, and 670,000 taxpayers account for 90 percent of all income taxes collected.

1939: The first Dairy Queen opens in Joliet, Ill.

1939: Nestle introduces the world's first instant coffee—Nescafe.

1939: The nation goes gaga over vitamins. The only over-the-counter products that outsell them are laxatives.

1939: The U.S. Department of Agriculture introduces the first food-stamp program to feed the needy, in Rochester, N.Y. The stamps moved surplus farm products into the homes of needy Americans.

ABOVE: A RIVETER IS AT WORK ON A CONSOLIDATED BOMBER AT THE CONSOLIDATED AIRCRAFT CORP, IN FORT WORTH, TEXAS, IN 1942.
Library of Congress

Every Soldier's emergency ration is three 4-oz. chocolate bars, known as D-Ration. These 3 bars sustain a fighting man for 24 hrs.—on beachheads and other "tough spots."

JOHNNY MARCHED OFF to war in the 1940s, and when he came home, it was to a country that would never be the same.

While he was gone, Jane marched off to the local factory. And she would never look at the kitchen, or her role in it, in the same way.

Although America was not yet in the war as the decade opened, many of our resources were already being directed toward use by our eventual Allies. The hard times of the depression faded as many found jobs in war-oriented plants. And the troubles abroad made other changes on the home front. Imports—things like spices—became scarce and expensive.

From posters and billboards to magazines, Americans were urged to conserve. In 1943 a *Better Homes and Gardens* article read, "Don't squander drippings—pour every dinky dab into a covered dish, store in refrigerator. Use for seasoning and shortening in muffins, spice cookies, gingerbread, corn bread and meat-pie toppers. Can't use it all? Strain it— pass it along for ammunition."

But American ingenuity was always at hand. Forever in love with technology, food processors thought the world was ready for a feast of dehydrated food. Manufacturers came up with dehydrated clam juice; dried spinach, beets, and potatoes; powdered eggs; and even dehydrated roasts and steaks. Cooks were willing to do their part doing the war years, but afterward, they wanted the real deal. The few foods that

MADE IN U.S.A.   No. 6787

NESTLÉ's CRUNCH

NESTLÉ's CRUNCH MILK CHOCOLATE

NESTLÉ's CRUNCH 1 oz.

PREPARED BY THE NESTLÉ COMPANY, INC., WHITE PLAINS, N.Y.
CONTAINS CRISPED RICE AND VANILLIN, AN ARTIFICIAL FLAVORING

NESTLÉ's makes the *Very Best* **CHOCOLATE!**

Nestle

Nestle

survived the craze were dried soups, puddings, and instant mashed potatoes.

After America entered the war, households became accustomed to planning meals around ration points. Rationed grocery items were assigned points and each person was granted 12 points a week. A pound of porterhouse steak in 1943 was 12 points, but a pound of ground beef was only seven points, leading to the popularity of meat loaf and stuffed peppers.

Chicken become more popular because it wasn't rationed, but it was expensive. Margarine and "salad oil" made from American corn were far more accessible than butter and imported olive oil were, and they became more important ingredients in the daily diet. Although sugar was rationed, home canners could get extra to "put up" the fruits of their Victory Gardens.

Americans had nothing on the suffering of Europeans, however.

Americans were allowed an average of 6 ounces of meat a day during the war; the English ration was 16 ounces a week. When the young Ted Koppel emigrated from England with his parents soon after the war, he was stunned by the advertisements for sweets and consumer goods in his new country. It would take years for a bombed-out Europe to return to normal.

When the war ended in 1945, America was ready for revelry. Millions of homes were built for returning GIs and their brides. Many households bought their first stoves, refrigerators, washing machines, and power lawn mowers.

Food had become more standardized

ABOVE: STEREOTYPES WERE TYPICAL ADVERTISING HOOKS WELL INTO THE MIDDLE OF THE CENTURY. THIS NATIONAL AD APPEARED IN 1948.

LEFT: SUDDENLY EVERYTHING IS INSTANT! INCLUDING THIS MINUTE RICE FROM 1948. Kraft

because of the military experience. Troops from California to New York had been served the same fare in mess halls, and that middle-of-the-road food became the norm. And, Americans had access to travel like never before, leading to the cookie-cutter fare of the Howard Johnsons and the White Castles of the highways.

Women looked at food differently, too. Having had a taste of the working world (and the freedom of not being tied to the kitchen), women jumped for convenience food. Canned fruits and vegetables were back, and new supermarkets were springing up in the nascent suburbs, taking much of the chore out of cooking.

Having made it through the savage economy of the 1930s and a brutal war in the 1940s, Americans were ready to enjoy the good life.

ABOVE: PLASTIC PRODUCTION SWITCHES TO MANUFACTURING HOME PRODUCTS FOLLOWING WORLD WAR II. Newell-Rubbermaid

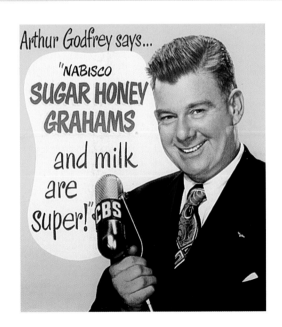

LEFT: ARTHUR GODFREY PUMPS FOR HONEY MAID GRAHAM CRACKERS VIA THE RADIO WAVES FROM 1946 TO 1955. Nabisco

Kraft

OREO®
CREME SANDWICH

ABOVE: This 1948 print ad is an indication of what is to come full force in the 1950s—advertising to children via the family's new television set. Nabisco

RIGHT: Salt marches on, but with a little more design and style. Morton's

OATS GO FULL CIRCLE

To THE GENERATION of Baby Boomers who grew up eating Cheerios, and then served it to their own children as one of their first finger foods, Cheerios may seem old-hat. But look back at the packages over the years and you'll see, oats have found it very hip to be round.

Called Cheeri Oats when introduced in 1941, it was the first ready-to-eat cereal based on oats. A "convenience" food, Cheeri Oats saved the housewife from sludging through a pot of hot oatmeal in the morning.

But by the 1950, the name had been changed to placate the country's largest oat packager. The Lone Ranger was close friends with the brand and hawked their wares via the radio. The 1960s saw a box that celebrated the future of space and at century's end, Millenios helped celebrate.

QUICKIE
CHICKEN AND NOODLES

[SERVES 6-8]

2 tablespoons oil or butter

7 ounces canned chicken meat

10-ounce can condensed mushroom soup

1 cup cooked peas

½ cup water

1 teaspoon salt

¼ teaspoon pepper

5 ounces egg noodles, cooked

MELT BUTTER or heat oil in saucepan. Stir in chicken, simmer but do not brown. Add mushroom soup, peas, water, and seasonings. Heat thoroughly, mix with noodles and serve hot.

— *Golden Anniversary Cook-Book* Fort Worth Macaroni Co. (O.B. Brand, 1949)

Where Field Kitchens Can't Reach, the "10-in-1" ration supplies food for 10 men for 1 day. A special chocolate bar is frequently in the dinner unit. Cocoa is a supper beverage.

ABOVE: NESTLE LAUNCHES ITS INSTANT
TEA, NESTEA, IN 1948. Nestle

RIGHT: A COUNTRY THAT, FOR
THE MOST PART, DIDN'T KNOW
ABOUT PARMESAN CHEESE 20
YEARS EARLIER GETS IT
ALREADY GRATED IN A CAN
IN 1945. Kraft

LEFT: FRANK SINATRA AND MODEL PEGGY LIPP SMILE FOR TOOTSIE ROLLS IN 1947. THE COMPANY PLANT IS IN HOBOKEN, N.J., SINATRA'S HOMETOWN.
Tootsie Roll Industries

BELOW RIGHT: DURING WORLD WAR II, ALL CANDY PRODUCTION GOES INTO MILITARY RATIONS. AMONG SOLDIERS, PER CAPITA CONSUMPTION HITS 50 POUNDS A YEAR, THREE TIMES THE PREWAR AVERAGE, ACCORDING TO THE NATIONAL CONFECTIONERS ASSOCIATION.

Nestle

Prisoner of War Packages, delivered by the Red Cross to homesick Americans in Axis prison camps, contain that nourishing reminder of home...one or more bars of chocolate.

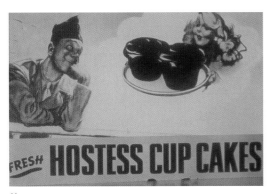

Hostess

Hershey

The Chocolate War

They're pretty savvy, those soldiers who run America's chocolate factories. Milton Hershey always refers to chocolate and candy as separate entities. Chocolate is healthy, nutritious, and full of energy.

In fact, that is what keeps his lines of supply open during World War II. When the government looked at rationing supplies for chocolate making, Hershey lobbies that chocolate is good for the troops. The National Confectioners Association, the marketing cooperative arm of the union of candy makers, spends $1 million in 1944 to advertise candy as the food that gives the military its energy.

During World War II, all candy production goes into military rations. Among soldiers, per capita consumption hits 50 pounds a year, three times the prewar average, according to the National Confectioners Association.

Hershey

Chocolate is a Fighting Food!

So supplies of chocolate products for those at home are limited.

If you can't always get your favorite Nestle's Chocolate Bar, Semi-Sweet Morsels or Ever-Ready Cocoa, remember your dealer's supply is restricted. The needs of our armed forces come first.

Return Flight Guaranteed!

Here, flying away by Government order, is Reynolds Wrap ... the pure aluminum foil that kept leftovers fresh, covered bowls so neatly and quickly, made roasting and baking so much easier and better. Aluminum foil is needed by the armed forces ... to protect rations, medical supplies, rustable parts and delicate instruments.

This protection is the more important because our supply lines are long, and because they must extend to whatever future fronts the defense of Freedom may require. The amount of aluminum used as "fighting foil" is small compared to the tons of aluminum in planes, ships, tanks, trucks, pontoon bridges, bazooka and other rocket tubes. But a first aid packet can be as vital as any weapon; all these needs have the same urgent priority.

For all this, and to restore civilian supply as soon as possible, the U.S. aluminum industry is rapidly expanding production. We face a double job: fighting shortages and inflation while we fight aggression. Reynolds is working at that double job *full time, full speed!*

Reynolds Metals Company, General Sales Offices, Louisville 1, Ky.

Reynolds Wrap is now "all out" for defense

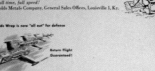

Return Flight
Guaranteed!

REYNOLDS ALUMINUM

Ad. No. 1M-1

This advertisement appears in:
Saturday Evening Post—May 5, 1951   U. S. News & World Report—April 20, 1951   McCalls—June, 1951
                                      Editor & Publisher—April 21, 1951   Better Homes & Gardens—June

ABOVE AND TOP RIGHT: ALL THE PRODUCE FROM THE NATION'S VICTORY GARDENS HAS TO BE "PUT UP" BY THE GROWERS OR, IF THEY WERE LUCKY, BY FRIENDS. A HOT, DEMANDING JOB IN THE DAYS BEFORE AIR-CONDITIONING, THIS MIGHT HAVE BEEN ONE OF THE STRONGEST HINTS TO WORKING WOMEN THAT SOMETHING WOULD HAVE TO GIVE. Library of Congress

CHAYOTE CON QUESO

[SERVES 4]

3 chayote squash

water

1 teaspoon sugar

1 teaspoon salt

Dash of pepper

3 tablespoons cream

1 tablespoon butter

¼ cup grated cheese

PEEL CHAYOTES and cut in thin slices. Cover with water and cook until tender. Drain. Add sugar, salt to taste, dash of pepper, and cream and butter. Add grated cheese; let melt and beat hard.

— Concha's *Mexican Kitchen Cook Book* by Catharine Ulmer Stoker (Naylor, 1946)

Library of Congress

LEFT AND BELOW: CALIFORNIA'S FRUIT AND VEGETABLE INDUSTRY THE NATION'S LARGEST, SUFFERED MIGHTILY WHEN JAPANESE-AMERICANS WERE FORCED TO RELOCATE TO CONFINED CAMPS DURING WORLD WAR II, ABANDONING FARMS AND BUSINESSES THEY HAD DEVELOPED.
Library of Congress

RIGHT: POST CONTINUES WITH ITS HEALTH-ORIENTED LINE OF CEREAL WITH THE 1942 INTRODUCTION OF RAISIN BRAN.
Kraft

Library of Congress

ABOVE: AMERICANS GO APPLIANCE CRAZY AFTER WORLD WAR II. THEY HAVE NEW MARRIAGES AND NEW HOMES AND WANT NEW APPLIANCES. MANUFACTURERS HAVE A DIFFICULT TIME KEEPING UP WITH DEMAND. THIS MODEL IS A 1940 MODEL, FILLED WITH MEAT AND BOTTLED MILK. Frigidaire

RIGHT: COULD THE WORLD GET ANY BETTER? SLICED CHEESE IS INTRODUCED IN 1949. Kraft

STOP-'EM-DEAD LOW-POINT
AFTER-CHURCH LUNCH MENU

MAY WINE BOWL

CREAM OF MUSHROOM SOUP

SLICED TONGUE WITH MUSTARD

MUSTARD SPINACH WITH NUTMEG AND LEMON

BAKED SHERRIED SWEET POTATOES

SPRING SALAD WITH MUSTARD FRENCH DRESSING

SOY BAKING POWDER BISCUITS

LIME SHERBET

COFFEE

— *House Beautiful* (May 1944)

ABOVE: FORMER FIRST LADY ELEANOR ROOSEVELT ATTENDS THE
FIRST PILLSBURY BAKE-OFF IN 1949 AND WRITES ABOUT IT IN
HER NEWSPAPER COLUMN. THE FIRST EVENT IS HOSTED BY ART
LINKLETTER SECOND FROM RIGHT. Pillsbury Bake-off

1940: One out of every five working women is a servant. Half are black or Hispanic.

1940: A&P supermarkets sell the first precut cellophane-wrapped meat.

1940: The first Dairy Queen opens in Joliet, Ill. First known for soft-serve ice cream, by 1950 there will be more than a thousand Dairy Queens across the country.

1940: M&M's are introduced in red, yellow, green, orange, brown, and violet. In 1949 tan replaces violet. During World War II, M&M's are part of GI rations.

Mars, Inc.

1941: President Roosevelt convenes the National Nutritional Conference for Defense to examine the causes of physical defects found in so many young men called up for the draft. Mayo Clinic nutrition expert Russell M. Wilder heads a group of experts to study the eating habits of 2,000 representative U.S. families.

1941: South Carolina is the first state to require enrichment of white bread with vitamins and iron.

1941: In January *Gourmet* magazine's first issue is published. The cover is a painting of a roasted boar's head.

1941: McCormick & Co. offers its first dehydrated products—onion flakes and parsley flakes.

1941: The safety of milk cartons is confirmed.

1941: James Beard's *Cook It Outdoors* is introduced in 1941. In 1954 he will publish Jim Beard's *Barbecue Cooking*.

1941: Cheerios are introduced.

1942: U.S. consumers hoard coffee, leading to a coffee ration of 1 pound every five weeks. Sugar is rationed; the weekly allowance is 8 ounces per person.

1942: Ideal weights are published by Metropolitan Life Insurance.

1942: American factories and the military push candy on workers and soldiers, believing its energy keeps them awake and effective. Lobbying by the National Candy Manufacturers helps the industry's cause.

1942: The frozen food industry grows as producers look for alternatives to metal cans during the war years.

1942: Victory Gardens sprout throughout the country as vegetables become scarce. They are especially hard to find in California because two-thirds of vegetables were brokered by Japanese-Americans, who have been relocated to internment camps. Forty percent of all vegetables are produced in almost 20 million Victory Gardens.

1942: The U.S. Army becomes the nation's largest candy customer. The Wrigley Co. packs K rations that contain canned meat, four cigarettes, compressed Graham biscuits, three tablets of sugar, and a stick of chewing gum.

Ration D is a 600-calorie Hershey bar (minus the cocoa butter so it won't melt) fortified with nutrients. The bar could also be "dissolved by crumbling into a cup of boiling water, if desired as a beverage."

Tootsie Roll Industries

1942: Tootsie Rolls also go off to war in ration kits and are a hit because they withstand severe weather conditions.

1943: Rubber, metal, paper, silk, and nylon are collected for recycling. Flour, fish, canned foods, and shoes are rationed.

1943: Ike Sewell and Ric Riccardo create Chicago-style (deep dish) pizza at Pizzeria Uno in Chicago.

1943: The sale of sliced bread is banned. Cheese and fat are rationed.

1943: Florence Brobeck, in her book *Cook It in a Casserole,* gives a low-ration-point recipe that combines canned tuna fish with cubed potatoes, peas, cheese, and white sauce.

1943: Recommended Daily Allowances for various nutrients are published for the first time. Health becomes a matter of patriotism as a notable number of inductees fail the military's physical. Public service posters push nutrition to a nation recovering from a depression when emphasis was not on what one ate, but how much one could afford to eat.

1943: Texas produce broker Gordon Harwell develops converted rice. Forrest Mars, owner of the Mars candy empire, buys the mill and soon, through the magic of advertising, the fictitious Uncle Ben becomes the leading brand of rice in the nation.

1943: A Trumanburger, named after Harry S, is concocted during the dying days of meat rationing. It includes baked beans.

1944: Meat, except steak, rationing ends after D-Day.

1944: The banana industry has been crippled since 1941 because the industry's ships are requisitioned by British and American governments. As the war winds down, in an effort to give bananas a designer label, the United Fruit Company creates Chiquita Banana, a banana-cum-Carmen Miranda- type Latin dancer. Chiquita, swinging hips samba-style, sings:

> *"I'm Chiquita Banana and I've come to say,*
> *"Bananas have to ripen in a certain way;*
> *"When they are flecked with brown and*
> *have a golden hue*
> *"Bananas taste the best and are the best for*
> *you."*

1945: Although many women lose their jobs when World War II ends and servicemen return home, the number of women in the workforce will never be as low as it was before the war.

1945: Toward the end of the year, food rationing of all items, except sugar, ends. Gasoline rationing also ends.

1945: American consumption of vegetables hits a record high because Victory Gardens supplant canned vegetables (the metal had been needed in the war effort).

1946: Pillsbury, a flour power since the 1800s, rolls out its first convenience baking product—pie crust mix. In 1955 the company does some of the mixing and introduces pie crust sticks.

1946: Earl W. Tupper invents resealable food containers. The inventor's plastic, a lightweight but sturdy "Poly-T," was probably first used in gas masks worn on European battlefields.

1946: Frozen french fried potatoes are introduced.

1947: Reynolds Metals Co. uses surplus aluminum from World War II to make Reynolds Wrap aluminum foil. The foil is packed in 25-foot-rolls, a size still used at the end of the century.

1947: U.S. sugar rationing ends, but President Harry Truman urges meat and egg conservation to save the grain for struggling Europeans.

1947: Refrigeration and the rise of suburbia are responsible for the creation of supermarkets, where all foodstuffs can be found under one roof.

1947: Pillsbury introduces hot roll mix.

1947: Reddi-Whip is the first major U.S. aerosol food product.

1947: Cake mixes first appear.

1947: McCormick & Co. acquires A. Schilling & Co., a San Francisco coffee, spice, and extract house in business since 1881. McCormick also forms an alliance with the Hernandez family to form McCormick de Mexico, S.A., of Mexico City.

1947: Marilyn Monroe is crowned the first Queen of the Artichokes.

1948: V8 Cocktail Vegetable Juice is introduced by Campbell Soup Co.

1948: Nestle introduces instant tea.

1948: 78 percent of U.S. homes have electricity provided by power stations.

1948: Dick and Mac McDonald cut the staff at the McDonald's in San Bernardino, Calif., and discover a fortune in self-service.

1948: The process of condensing and freezing orange juice is developed. But the Minute Maid Co. needs help in getting the word out. Investor John Hay Whitney offers a glass to his golf partner, Bing Crosby. Crosby loves it, buys 20,000 shares of the company, and hawks the juice on radio and television. Demand for Florida orange juice quadruples.

1949: Sara Lee Cheese Cake is introduced by baker Charles Lubin, who names the product for his daughter.

1949: About 70 percent of U.S. milk is homogenized, compared with 33 percent in 1940.

1949: The first Pillsbury Bake-Off Contest, called the Grand National Baking and Recipe Contest, takes place at New York's Waldorf-Astoria Hotel. Former first lady Eleanor Roosevelt attends and writes about the contest in her newspaper column. "This is a healthy contest and a highly American one. It may sell Pillsbury flour but it also reaches far down into the lives of the housewives of America. These are women who ran their homes and cooked at home. They were not professional cooks."

1949: Fritos Corn Chips are introduced nationally.

1949: The electric dishwasher debuts, but is not a household word until the late 1960s, when sales top 2 million units.

ABOVE: ALTHOUGH RAYTHEON INTRODUCED THE FIRST MICROWAVE OVEN FOR COOKING IN 1947, THE OVEN'S LARGE SIZE AND CURIOUS SCIENCE RELEGATED THEM TO INSTITUTIONAL APPLICATIONS LIKE PASSENGER TRAINS THAT PROVIDED FOOD SERVICE. Raytheon

POSTWAR AFFLUENCE EXPANDS American palates and launches the age of convenience foods.

In the 1950s, America likes Ike and just about everything else. The conquering heroes had come home. With the help of the GI Bill, they earned educations. They married, they had some babies, and with more help from the GI Bill, they bought 3-1-1 homes in the sprouting suburbs.

When the decade opened, 21.6 percent of wives worked outside the home. By 1960 that number hit 30.5 percent. The reason for the jump? There was simply so much to buy. Cars and refrigerators and televisions and washing machines cost money. And after a couple of decades of doing without—a depression followed by a war—America was ready for the good life.

I Love Lucy was the sweetheart of the country—introducing Middle America to Babalu and situation comedy. It was a good-feeling show for a good-feeling time. Another TV series reflected the darker side of the decade. I *Led Three Lives* was the tale of Herbert A. Philbrick, a Boston ad man by day, a member of the Communist Party by night, and an FBI agent in his remaining work hours.

TV was pervasive. A recipe for clam dip appeared on *The Kraft Music Hall,* a variety show. Within 24 hours, the grocery shelves in New York City were stripped of canned clams.

The popularity of television led to the introduction of the TV dinner in 1954. The first production order was for 5,000 dinners, thought to be

Nabisco

a big gamble at the time. The company sold 10 million dinners that year. When the dinners were introduced, few people owned freezers. Most dinners were bought and eaten the same day.

And to further relieve Mom of some homemaking stress, Dad often matched meat with flame in the backyard. Backyards became the public squares of the suburbs. June and Ward would come over with the kids, and while the kids played with their Hula Hoops and shot cap pistols, Dad burned dinner.

If that wasn't enough help for Mom, the supermarket was nearby. By 1952 the average U.S. grocery stocked 4,000 items, a leap from about 870 in 1928. By the mid-1960s, that number was up to 8,000 items.

Ladies Home Journal Food Editor Poppy Cannon lent a hand with her *The New Can-Opener Cookbook.* Canned, frozen, and foods in jars, were still the cutting edge of food technology.

But underneath, something else was brewing. American men had traveled, and although it wasn't under the best conditions, it exposed them to a world of food beyond Mom's meatloaf and the dinners of like-minded neighbors. And Americans were mobile in their new cars, taking vacations and relocating for jobs away from farms. That, too, led to exposure to new experiences and flavors.

There was money for vacations, and that often meant money for restaurant meals. Certainly, a lot of those restaurants were the Howard Johnson's of the dining world, and certainly, few of them were the restaurants of the elite—Le Pavillon in New York City, the Pump Room in Chicago. But the average Joe was seeing the world, and he was hungry for more.

Yessiree, Bob.

LEFT: RAY KROC,
A CHICAGO-BASED
MILK SHAKE MACHINE
DISTRIBUTOR, OPENS
HIS FIRST MCDONALD'S
IN DES PLAINES, ILL.,
IN 1955. BY THIS TIME,
THE GOLDEN ARCHES
ARE A PART OF THE
ARCHITECTURE. IN 1961
KROC BOUGHT OUT THE
MCDONALDS FOR $2.7
MILLION. McDonald's Corp.

ABOVE: CRACKER BARREL
CHEESE, "AGED FOR 60 DAYS,"
IS INTRODUCED IN 1954. Kraft

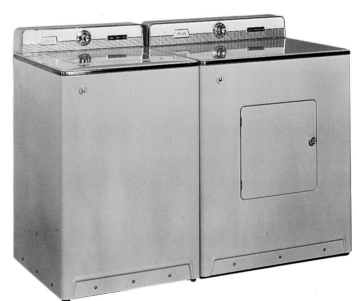

ABOVE: THE DEPENDIBILITY PEOPLE BEGAN
COLORIZING SOME OF THEIR WASHERS
AND DRYERS IN 1954. FIRST THEY ROLLED
OUT PASTEL GREEN SUPERMATICS, THEN
YELLOW, AND FINALLY THIS MAMIE
EISENHOWER PINK ENSEMBLE. Maytag

Cake mixes from General Mills (Betty Crocker) and Pillsbury start appearing at the end of the 1940s. The first mix is for a single-layer ginger cake, followed by the now-standard devil's food layer cake. Then a white layer cake mix made its appears, followed by a chocolate fudge cake mix.

I guarantee a perfect devils food cake

Although many women are at home with new families, many decide to stay in the workforce, and 35 cents for cake mix is well worth the convenience.

The two pioneering companies miscalculate by including powdered eggs in the mixes. Consumers make it clear they want to add their own eggs—these are, after all, people who had cooked in the recent past. So, with a quick turn-around, mixes are reformulated.

Pillsbury introduces angel food cake mix. General Mills formulates the chiffon cake.

When Duncan Hines enters the market in 1951, it is with a rousing success. The company's Three Star Surprise, one mix that could be turned into three flavors, captures 48 percent of the market in three weeks.

In 1954 Betty Crocker introduces, for smaller families, the Answer Cake—a pan, mix, and frosting in one package. Betty Crocker drops that item in 1968, but in 1975 introduces Stir 'n Frost, a cake mix, pan, and ready-to-spread frosting in one box.

In the 1970s, cakes using pudding mixes become the rage among home bakers. Pillsbury is the first out of the blocks with this one, introducing pudding-in-the-mix layer cakes in 1979.

The 1990s see microwave and lower-fat cake mixes. Frosting mixes almost disappear from the shelves; instead, home bakers use prepared frosting sold in a peel-open plastic tub.

"I GUARANTEE: A perfect cake every time you bake...cake...after cake...after cake"

Betty Crocker

"Let's have a pink party... it's so easy with my White Cake mix."

Betty Crocker CAKE MIXES

Try These Wonderful Betty Crocker Cake Mixes •WHITE •YELLOW •CHOCOLATE DEVILS FOOD •HONEY SPICE •GINGER BREAD

KRAFT MUSIC HALL
CLAM APPETIZER DIP

[YIELDS 1 1/2 CUPS]

6¼-ounce can minced clams, undrained

8-ounce package PHILADELPHIA Cream Cheese, softened

2 teaspoons lemon juice

1½ teaspoons Worcestershire sauce

¼ teaspoon garlic salt

Dash pepper

DRAIN CLAMS, reserving ¼ cup liquid.
Mix clams, reserved liquid, and remaining ingredients until well blended.
Refrigerate.
Serve with potato chips or vegetable dippers.

— Kraft

TAO BEAN SPROUTS

[SERVES 4]

1 pound canned bean sprouts

1 tablespoon butter or peanut oil

4-ounce can mushroom pieces with their own liquid

¼ teaspoon salt

Freshly ground black pepper

Chopped cashews

DRAIN BEAN sprouts. Rinse in cold water.
Heat a well-greased frying pan over high heat. Add butter or peanut oil, the mushroom pieces with their liquid, and the salt. Stir and fry about 1 minute or until well-heated. Add bean sprouts, cover, and cook 2 minutes longer. Sprinkle with freshly ground black pepper. Scatter nuts over top. Serve immediately.

— *The New Can-Opener Cookbook* by Poppy Cannon (Crowell, 1951)

PUT A LID ON IT

IN 1946 Earl W. Tupper invents resealable food containers. The inventor's plastic, a lightweight but sturdy "Poly-T," was probably first used in gas masks worn on European battlefields.

After the war, soldiers were coming home, getting married, buying homes, and outfitting them with appliances. Those who were affluent enough to have had refrigerators before the war didn't yet have the little helpers that would change the way they looked at leftovers.

Before the plastics boom, consumers used clunky glass "refrigerator boxes" or crockery to store food in the refrigerator. Both were unwieldy space eaters, and they didn't keep food particularly fresh.

But Tupperware's plastic was just about indestructible, and the airtight seals (modeled after paint can rims) were ideal for sealing in freshness. And this generation, after all, was not yet accustomed to the disposable world to come. It managed to keep track of the lids.

Despite Tupperware's advantages, it was a hard sell in standard retail outlets. Consumers needed to see how it worked. However, one Brownie Wise, a go-getter single mother, came up with the idea of parties in homes to demonstrate the product. In 1948 Tupperware held its first home party—a product demonstration and refreshments all in one.

By 1951 Tupperware pulls its products from stores and begins selling exclusively through home parties. It's a concept that is ideal for the new breed of homemaker. She has appliances to ease her housework burden, but she's in a new suburb and work outside the home is not an option. She can go to Tupperware parties to socialize with other women, or, if she'd rather, she can give the parties and make a little income of her own.

We're going to have a party
With games and prizes, too;
And the miracle of Tupperware
Demonstrated just for you!

With hints on how to store your food,
And tips on food preserving,
This special kind of party
Of your time is well deserving.

So come, enjoy my party
(Of course you are invited)
Let me know that you'll be there,
I know you'll be excited!

EVERETT, MAR 15 4 PM 1953

LEFT: TUPPERWARE PARTIES WERE A WAY FOR WOMEN IN THE SUBURBS TO SOCIALIZE, NOW THAT MANY OF THEM WERE LIVING AWAY FROM THE NUCLEAR FAMILIES THAT HAD BOUND COMMUNITIES BEFORE WORLD WAR II. WITH THEIR CHILDREN IN SCHOOL, AND THEIR HUSBANDS AT WORK, WOMEN HAD MORE LEISURE TIME THAN THEIR MOTHERS' MANAGED—THANKS TO HOUSES FULL OF APPLIANCES AND CONVENIENCES SUCH A READY-MADE SOAP, A LUXURY TO MANY OF THEIR GRANDMOTHERS.

Tupperware Home Parties

TUPPERWARE

The old and new of the Tupperware parade of products. At top left is an egg slicer, a 1990s design that might have made a 1950s homemaker think of Martians. At bottom right is another 1990s design, a grater for authentic Parmesan cheese. Advertising in the 1960s, however, still relied on fantasy and romance with orchids afloat in "burpable" bowls. At top right is a postcard a Tupperware party giver would send as an invitation for a hours of socializing and soft selling of household wares.

Amazing!

First second—
cold milk

—next second
stir in Quik

NESTLÉ's
Quik
DELICIOUS
CHOCOLATE
FLAVOR

and you get
RICH CHOCOLATY
MILK...M-M\M

—instantly with
NESTLÉ's
Quik!

...the fastest you ever
mixed—the best you ever
tasted! Because this amazing
new Quik *mixes with cold milk*—
INSTANTLY! No beating...no
bother...and *no* refrigerating!
Just stir and serve!
P.S.----It *stays* chocolaty
all the way through!

REG. U.S. PAT. OFF.

JUST ADD MILK
MAKES ONE PINT
4 OZ. NET WT. • 113 GM.

JELL-O
BRAND
New
INSTANT PUDDING
No Cooking
CHOCOLATE
FLAVOR

NEW 'BUSY-DAY' DESSERT

—you can make and serve it
at the **very** **last** **minute!**

SPEEDY! Fix it right at dessert time.
No waiting—it's instant!

SIMPLE! No cooking. Just add to milk,
whip 1 minute.

SWELL! Wonderful, new texture...
light 'n fluffy. Nourishing
for kids.

KEEP IT HANDY! Ready on your shelf for last minute
making on all your busy days!

JELL-O
New
INSTANT PUDDING
No Cooking
CHOCOLATE

VANILLA
CHOCOLATE
BUTTERSCOTCH

JELL-O IS A REGISTERED TRADEMARK OF GENERAL FOODS CORPORATION

BEEF
STROGANOFF

[Serves 4]

1½ cups uncooked bow tie pasta

1 pound beef top sirloin steak

salt

pepper

½ pound mushrooms, cut into ½-inch slices

⅓ cup coarsely chopped onion

2 teaspoons vegetable oil

1 to 2 tablespoons all purpose flour

¾ cup beef broth

1 tablespoon sliced green onion

¼ cup sour cream

COOK PASTA according to package directions. Meanwhile, trim fat from beef and cut into ½-inch cubes. Spray large nonstick skillet with vegetable cooking spray. Heat skillet over medium-high heat until hot. Add half of the beef and stir-fry 1–2 minutes or until outside surface is no longer pink. Season with salt and pepper if desired. Remove from skillet and keep warm.

Repeat with remaining beef.

In same skillet, cook mushrooms and onion in oil 2 minutes or until tender.

Stir in flour. Gradually add broth, stirring until blended. Bring to a boil. Cook and stir 2 minutes.

Return beef to skillet and heat through.

Serve beef mixture over pasta. Sprinkle with green onion and serve with sour cream to dollop on top.

— Texas Beef Council

RIGHT: RONALD REAGAN'S HEALTHY IMAGE WORKS WITH A V-8 VEGETABLE JUICE PROMOTION IN 1958.
Campbell Soup Co.

RIGHT: CHEEZ WHIZ, JARRED PASTEURIZED
PROCESS CHEESE SPREAD, IS INTRODUCED IN
1953 IN A PRY-TOP JAR. IN 1992 KRAFT
INTRODUCES A LOWER FAT VERSION. CHEEZ
WHIZ IS THE BUTT OF GENERATIONS OF
JOKES, BUT IT'S DE RIGUEUR ON CELERY
STICKS AT HOLIDAYS. BROCCOLI, BURIED
UNDER A LAYER OF MELTED CHEEZ WHIZ,
BECOMES ONE OF MOTHER'S LITTLE HELPERS.

LEFT AND BELOW:
REYNOLDS WRAP HELPS AT
HOME IN THE 1950S, BUT
ONCE AGAIN IT BECOMES
EMBROILED IN COMBAT
DURING THE KOREAN
CONFLICT. PATRIOTIC
SHOPPERS GIVE UP THEIR
FOOD STORAGE HELPER,
FOR A SHORT WHILE, SO
REYNOLDS COULD GO OFF
TO WAR. Reynold's

THE GIRL IN THE MOON IMAGE SELLS BEER
FOR MILLER FOR MORE THAN 50 YEARS. AT
LEFT, SHE APPEARS ON A TRAY AS SHE
LOOKED FROM 1903 TO 1919. AT RIGHT,
SHE'S SHOWING MORE SKIN IN THE LATE
1940S AND EARLY 1950S. Miller Brewing Co.

Say "**CHARGE IT**" At any of the fine restaurants listed below!

You don't have to be a top executive to enjoy the many benefits of this man-about-town charge account privilege. Any responsible business man or woman, executive or employe, can have this Diners' Club Card simply by applying by mail or phone today for an application and further particulars!

Yes, your Diners' Club Card is a master credit card at these and one hundred other superb eating places in the metropolitan New York area, Chicago and other key cities. Receive one monthly statement reflecting all charges.

DINERS' CLUB

Empire State Building, N. Y. C. • BRyant 9-2160

FRANCIS X. MCNAMARA IS UNABLE TO PAY FOR
A RESTAURANT MEAL IN NEW YORK CITY. HIS
PREDICAMENT GIVES HIM THE IDEA FOR DINERS
CLUB—A CHARGE CARD FOR RESTAURANTS.
© Diner's Club

BARBECUED COUNTRY RIBS

[SERVES 8]

½ cup red wine vinegar

¼ cup vegetable oil

½ cup tomato sauce

1 tablespoon chili powder

2 teaspoons seasoning salt

2 teaspoons Salad Supreme

1 teaspoon celery seed

1 teaspoon lemon and pepper seasoning salt

½ teaspoon ground cumin

5 pounds country-style pork ribs

COMBINE ALL ingredients except ribs and mix well. Cut ribs in large serving pieces and place in plastic bag. Add oil-vinegar mixture and close bag. Chill 2 hours or longer, turning the bag occasionally so marinade covers meat. When ready to cook, drain, saving the marinade. Grill slowly about 8 inches from coals, 40 minutes or until well done, turning and basting frequently (about every 5 to 8 minutes) with marinade.

— McCormick

ABOVE: THE FIRST McDONALD'S OPENS BY BROTHERS RICHARD AND MAURICE McDONALD IN SAN BERNARDINO, CALIF., JUST BEFORE WORLD WAR II. BUT IT IS AFTER THEY FIRE THE CARHOPS, CUT THE PRICES IN HALF, AND REQUIRE CUSTOMERS TO ORDER AT THE WINDOW THAT THEIR BUSINESS EXPLODES. McDonald's Corp.

LEFT: A MODEL SHOWS A 1957 FRIGIDAIRE REFRIGERATOR. IN THE 1950S, THE COMPANY INTRODUCES ITS FIRST FAMILY OF APPLIANCES IN MATCHING COLORS AND THE FIRST FROST-PROOF REFRIGERATOR THAT ELIMINATES DEFROSTING. Frigidaire

BELOW: TANG BREAKFAST BEVERAGE CRYSTALS, AN ORANGE-FLAVOR POWDERED DRINK MIX, IS INTRODUCED NATIONALLY IN 1958. CONTRARY TO PLAYGROUND MYTH, TANG IS NOT INVENTED FOR THE ASTRONAUTS, ALTHOUGH IT DOES GO INTO SPACE WITH GEMINI 4 IN 1965 AND ON ALL MANNED U.S. FLIGHTS THROUGHOUT THE REST OF THE CENTURY. Kraft

LEFT: IN THE GREAT AMERICAN CONSUMER TRADITION, S&H GREEN STAMPS REWARDED SHOPPERS FOR SPENDING MONEY. THOMAS SPERRY AND SHELLEY HUTCHINSON FOUNDED S&H IN 1896 BUT THE COMPANY REACHED ITS HEIGHT OF POPULARITY IN THE 1960S WHEN CONSUMERS TRADED PILES OF BOOKLETS FILLED WITH S&H GREEN STAMPS FOR GOODS LIKE CARD TABLES AND TV TRAYS. CONSUMERS RECEIVED THE STAMPS IN EXCHANGE FOR DOING BUSINESS WITH EVERYONE FROM THE CORNER GAS STATION TO THE NEIGHBORHOOD SUPERMARKET. IN 1964, RESIDENTS OF ERIE, PA., TRADED IN 4,500 BOOKS OF GREEN STAMPS IN EXCHANGE FOR A PAIR OF GORILLAS FOR THE LOCAL ZOO.

THE HOME OF RALPH SR. AND SUNNY WILSON IN
TEMPLE, TEXAS, IS A TESTING GROUND FOR
LAMINATES—MANUFACTURED SURFACES—RENDERED
HERE IN VIBRANT 1950S COLORS. IN ADDITION TO
BEING A SHOWROOM FOR RALPH'S COMPANY,
WILSONART INTERNATIONAL, THIS HOUSE ON THE
NATIONAL HISTORIC REGISTER IS A VIBRANT
EXAMPLE OF 1950S ESTHETICS. THE FLOOR PLAN IS
OPEN, WITHOUT CONFINED FORMAL SPACES, AND
IS THE IDEAL SETTING FOR THE ENTERTAINMENT
FORMATS OF THE AGE—BARBECUES AND COCKTAIL
PARTIES. Wilsonart International

1950: Sugar Pops are introduced.

1950: Francis X. McNamara is unable to pay for a restaurant meal in New York City because he forgot his money. This spurs him to create the Diners Club. For $3 a year, cardholders could charge their meals at 27 restaurants in the city. By the end of 1951, more than $1 million is charged on the new card.

© Diner's Club

1950: Lawry's introduces its Seasoned Salt.

1950: In Quincy, Mass., Bill Rosenberg changes the name of his doughnut shop to Dunkin' Donuts. In 1955 he sells his first franchise.

1950: Ellen Gordon, 18, appears in a Tootsie Roll ad in *Life* magazine. In 1978 she is named president of the company, the second woman to be named president of a company listed on the New York Stock Exchange. Gordon's father supplies packaging to the company before the depression and eventually acquires it when Tootsie Roll has trouble paying its bills. The company's main plant in Chicago is where the ill-fated Tucker auto-mobile was produced.

1950: The rest of America (outside California, Hawaii—then a U.S. territory—and Florida) starts using avocados in salads.

1950: Minute Rice is introduced.

1951: *I Love Lucy* debuts on CBS.

1951: The first Jack-in-the-Box opens in San Diego.

1951: Former Marine Glen Bell, 28, introduces the first fast-food taco at his hamburger and hot dog stand in San Bernardino, Calif. The town is home to orchards, railroad yards, an air force base—and the original and very popular McDonald's. Bell, looking for a unique product, spots tacos at an area restaurant. He comes up with a contraption that will hold tortillas in hot oil to form the now-classic U-shaped taco shell—enabling him to pre-fry tortillas and offer fast Mexican fare.

1951: S&H Green Stamps get their start at the Denver store chain King Sooper.

1951: The defense industry needs aluminum for the Korean War effort, so Reynolds curtails production of its wrap for home use.

1951: Tropicana orange and grapefruit juices are introduced.

1952: Colonel Sanders sells its first Kentucky Fried Chicken franchise.

1952: Pream, the powdered nondairy coffee "cream" is introduced.

1952: The Lipton food company rolls out a dehydrated onion soup mix that will earn its fame as a base for onion dip: 2 envelopes of mix plus 1 cup sour cream. Lipton eventually prints the recipe, "California Dip," on the package.

1952: Pillsbury and Boise Cascade develop and patent the "crack on the black line" technique for opening tubes of refrigerated dough.

1952: Mrs. Paul's introduces fish sticks.

1952: Kellogg's Sugar Frosted Flakes are introduced.

1952: George Stephen, frustrated with barbecuing on an open-broiler grill, decides to develop a better barbecue grill. He works for a metal works company in Chicago, so he has experience shaping metal. His sales to friends and neighbors go so well that by the end of the decade he buys out the barbecue division of Weber Brothers Metal Works and creates Weber-Stephen Products Co.

1952: All things western are the rage, from coonskin hats to cowboy-theme chenille bedspreads to Roy Rogers Family Restaurants.

1953: Swift begins an aggressive program to develop a better turkey. (Turkey has been marketed since 1900, but it's a dark, chewy bird with tough tendons and a lot of pin feathers.) The company, with the help of genetics, develops a broad-breasted bird without the tough tendons and uses hot-water baths to remove feathers. In 1954 the Butterball brand and the self-basting turkey are introduced.

1953: Reynolds is again manufacturing aluminum foil for consumers. Saran Wrap is introduced.

1953: The French Sardine Co. (in existence since 1917) becomes Star-Kist Foods.

1953: Eggo Frozen Waffles are introduced.

1953: Fritos introduces The Frito Kid, a mascot the company uses until 1967.

1953: Cheez Whiz is introduced as a shortcut for homemakers making Welsh rarebit. Children come up with far more imaginative uses.

Frito-Lay

1954: The C.A. Swanson Co. has a problem. The holidays are over, but they still have railroad cars full of frozen turkeys. Americans eat turkey at Thanksgiving and Christmas, and a frozen turkey isn't going to hold until the next go-round of family celebrations.

Employee Gerry Thomas has an idea (although fellow workers nearly laugh him out of the Omaha plant): package the turkey, along with some dressing, gravy, cornbread, peas, and sweet potatoes into a partitioned metal tray. Sell it frozen, and consumers could heat it up for dinner. His name for the leftover meal: TV Dinner.

Swanson made fewer than 6,000 of the 98-cent meals. Within a year they had shipped 10 million more.

At the end of the century, Swanson still turns out the meals, and the most popular flavor is still turkey.

1954: The first Burger King opens in Miami. A burger is 18 cents, as is a milkshake. The Whopper is introduced in 1957 and sells for 37 cents.

1954: General Electric introduces the first automatic portable dishwasher, the Mobile Maid.

1954: During the decade McCormick adds saffron, barbecue spice, sesame seeds, Italian seasoning, dehydrated dip mix, Clamato juice, and foil-lined pouch packaging to its product line.

1954: Jonas Salk's polio vaccine is proven safe and effective, and the first successful kidney transplant is performed.

1954: Peanut M&M's are introduced.

1955: "Food is perhaps America's biggest weapon in the Cold War," writes *Life* magazine in January, saying that the $73 billion food basket created and consumed each year is "America's biggest business."

1955: Milkshake-machine salesman Ray Kroc tries to persuade Dick and Mac McDonald (owners of the original McDonald's in California) to franchise their concept. They aren't interested, but they tell Kroc to go ahead and try his hand. Kroc opens his first restaurant in Des Plaines, Ill., and eventually buys out the McDonalds.

1956: *Good Housekeeping* runs a recipe for Man-Winning Tomato Salad in its September issue.

1956: The U.S. Department of Agriculture formulates the four basic food groups.

1956: Jif Peanut Butter is introduced.

1956: Certs, the first candy breath mint, is introduced.

1956: More than 80 percent of U.S. households have refrigerators. By contrast, only 8 percent of British households have refrigerators.

1957: The first patent for Pam nonstick cooking spray is issued.

General Electric

1957: *Better Homes and Gardens* prints its first microwave-cooking article.

1957: Kikkoman Soy Sauce is sold in the U.S.

1957: Margarine sales take the lead over butter.

1957: Williams-Sonoma opens in San Francisco.

1957: Pillsbury introduces refrigerated cookie dough.

1957: The first Baggies and sandwich bags on a roll are introduced.

1958: Rice-A-Roni debuts.

1958: Ruffles Potato Chips, made from a thin-skinned potato and with a specially designed blade, are introduced. Ideal for au courant dips, by the end of the century they're generating more than $1 billion a year in sales for their parent company, Frito-Lay.

1958: Eighteen-year-old Frank Carney sees a story in the *Saturday Evening Post* about the pizza fad among teenagers and college students. With $600 borrowed from his mother, he opens the first Pizza Hut in Wichita, Kan.

1958: The German chocolate cake recipe is printed on Baker's Sweet Chocolate wrappers.

1958: Tang Breakfast Beverage Crystals is introduced nationally.

1959: At a special showing of a U.S. model kitchen in Moscow, Vice President Richard Nixon, in a debate with Soviet Premier Nikita Khrushchev, upholds the U.S. food system as the "showcase for democracy." (The meeting will forever be known as the "kitchen debate.") The two end their confrontation by drinking several bottles of Pepsi-Cola together. Pepsi wins exclusive rights to sell cola in the U.S.S.R. But Coca-Cola conducts an investigation and finds that Nixon was once offered the presidency of a foreign division of Pepsi and had been a lawyer for Pepsi while practicing in New York City.

1959: Häagen-Dazs ice cream is introduced.

I N THE 1960S, gourmet was groovy, Pop-Tarts popped up, and Julia Child brought French cooking home. The 1960s were as tumultuous at the table as they were on college campuses and on the streets.

The decade started graciously enough. The prosperous but stodgy 1950s seemed officially over when Ike and Mamie left the White House and Jack and Jackie moved in. Gone were the golf holidays and Ike puttering over a hot plate in the residence. In were glamour, youth, and the first French chef in the country's first mansion.

Those of us who wanted to try some of those Kennedy-esque dishes at home had Julia Child as our first guide. Child was well into middle age when she first appeared on Boston public television, but she clearly sparked the country's nascent interest in French food. A California native who had traveled the world with her diplomat husband, Child brought just the right amount of humor to haute cuisine to make it palatable to the American cook.

As we sent our first man into space, many of us also experienced our first trip abroad. Europe was in, thanks to the Beatles, the Volkswagen, and affordable air travel.

But the 1960s weren't all about pot-au-feu and champagne. They were also about Pringles and Cold Duck. We may love the cachet of the Continent, but convenience will always be king. The 1960s gave us Maxim freeze-dried coffee, Awake synthetic orange juice, and Kaboom breakfast food (43.8 percent sugar).

By 1960, 30.5 percent of married women

were working outside the home, and by 1965, 35 percent of the entire work force was female. Along with Twiggy and *That Girl,* being single was sexy. *Playboy* and *Cosmopolitan*'s Helen Gurley Brown published cookbooks to help this emerging market.

The 1960s also gave us the health-food movement sparked by Rachel Carson's examination of environmental pollution and the hippie lifestyle of communal, back-to-nature living. And you could get everything you wanted at "Alice's Restaurant," exceptin' Alice.

The hungry and the disenfranchised made their plights public with lunch-counter sit-ins and the Poor People's March on Washington. Cultural pride appeared with soul-food restaurants and contests like the Washington Natural Gas Co.'s first Soul Food Recipe Contest in 1969.

Food, again, was about our future and our past.

ABOVE: POP TARTS—PASTRY FROM A TOASTER—ARE INTRODUCED IN 1964. Kraft

LEFT: HOSTESS INTRODUCES DING DONGS IN 1967, NAMING THE SNACK CAKE AFTER THE CHIMING BELLS IN ITS FIRST TELEVISION COMMERCIAL. TO AVOID CONFUSION WITH OTHER BRANDS, THE CAKES ARE CALLED DING DONGS IN THE WEST AND MIDWEST, BUT IN THE EAST THEY'RE KING DONS. IN OTHER REGIONS THEY'RE CALLED BIG WHEELS. EVENTUALLY, THEY'RE ALL NAMED DING DONGS. KING DING DONG BECOMES THE MASCOT IN 1970. Hostess

Consumer Reports – consumer advocate

A ZEALOUS ENGINEER, an equally zealous staff, and a drive to survive combine to create Consumer Reports, a watchdog organization that still works to inform and protect Americans.

In 1926 engineer Frederick Schlink organizes a consumer club in White Plains, N.Y. The club distributes lists and recommendations concerning the onslaught of consumer products coming to market. Schlink even writes a book, *Your Money's Worth*, which leads to the founding of Consumers' Reasearch and the *Consumers' Research Bulletin*.

Consumers Union

Schlink and director of Consumers' Research Arthur Kallet publish *100,000,000 Guinea Pigs: Dangers in Everyday Foods, Drugs and Cosmetics* in 1933. They also move the operation to rural Washington, N.J. The bucolic setting, long hours, and low pay don't sit well with the journalists and engineers who have relocated from New York City. In 1935 the workers strike—and Schlink calls them "red."

In 1936 the workers receive a charter from the state of New York and begin *Consumers Union Reports*, the May issue of which examines Grade A and Grade B milk, breakfast cereals, soup, and nylon stockings. Circulation is a mere 4,000.

Starting with little money and not accepting advertising, *Consumers Union Reports* has a rough beginning. By 1941 innovations in consumer products are dwindling because of the war effort. In 1942 the magazine changes its name to *Consumer Reports* to deemphasize the union handle.

The end of the war brings G.I.s home to new houses, new families, new appliances, and, in many cases, their first look at this "new" magazine. In 1950 subscriptions to *Consumer Reports* reach almost 400,000.

The Consumer Reports organization leads the way in examining American consumer goods. In 1953 it tests the components of cigarettes. In 1954 it rates color televisions. In 1962 it publishes a special edition of *Silent Spring*. In 1974 it publishes an award-winning series on the contamination of U.S. water.

By 1992 *Consumer Reports* magazine boasts a paid circulation list of 5 million subscribers, one of the largest magazine circulations in the nation.

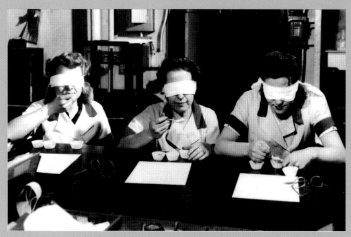

Consumers Union

In 1945, CONSUMER REPORTS taste gelatin and pudding packaged desserts, writing, "These packaged desserts do enable the busy housewife to whip together a more or-less tasty dessert in a very few minutes." However, the testers find that anything colored red is just as likely to be called cherry, raspberry, or strawberry. And even lemon and lime were mistaken for strawberry.

In 1952 the company checks out home freezers. The magazine has a few problems with the Kelvinator FR-63. Items on the bottom are difficult to reach and the lid could slam down on your head or your hand.

ABOVE: BROTHERS TOM AND JAMES MONAGHAN
PURCHASE DOMINICK'S, A PIZZA STORE IN YPSILANTI,
MICH. IN 1961 JAMES TRADES HIS HALF OF THE
BUSINESS TO HIS BROTHER FOR A VOLKSWAGEN
BEETLE. IN 1965 TOM RENAMES THE BUSINESS
DOMINO'S PIZZA. Domino's Pizza

ABOVE: TRIX ARE
FOR KIDS IN THE
1960S. General Mills

LEFT: MCDONALD'S ROLLS OUT THE
BIG MAC NATIONALLY IN 1968. THE
PRODUCT IS THE IDEA OF ONE OF THE
COMPANY'S EARLIEST FRANCHISEES,
WHO HAD A DOZEN STORES IN
PITTSBURGH. McDonald's Corp.

Interstate Bakeries Corp.

In 1960 four African-American freshmen from North Carolina Agricultural and Technical College in Greensboro walk into the F. W. Woolworth store and sit at the lunch counter. They are not served but they stay until closing time. The next morning, they return with 25 students. Within 2 weeks similar sit-ins spread to several cities. Within a year demonstrations are staged in more than 100 cities. Ronald Martin, Robert Patterson, and Mark Martin stage a sit-down strike after being refused service at the F.W. Woolworth luncheon counter, Greensboro, N.C., 1960. Library of Congress

PICKLED SHRIMP APPETIZER

[SERVES 8–10]

2½ to 3 pounds shrimp, boiled in seasoned water or crab boil

Sliced onions

7–8 bay leaves

SAUCE

1¼ cups vegetable oil

¾ cup vinegar

1½ teaspoons salt

2½ teaspoons celery seed

2½ tablespoons capers and juice

Dash of Tabasco

PEEL SHRIMP, leaving tails on if desired. In glass jar, alternate layers of shrimp and sliced onions. Top with the bay leaves. Combine sauce ingredients and pour over shrimp. Marinate in refrigerator for 2 days before serving.

— *Heavenly Cooking From Space City U.S.A.*
by Sisterhood Temple Beth Israel, Houston (Premier, 1967)

ABOVE: THE FIRST CRATE AND BARREL IS LOCATED IN CHICAGO'S OLD TOWN. THE WIDE USE OF HOME DISHWASHERS CAUSES FINE CHINA SALES TO PLUMMET. INSTEAD, CONSUMERS TURN TO STONEWARE AND ECLECTIC SERVING DISHES. Crate and Barrel

AMERICAN FOOD
MANUFACTURERS,
NEVER KNOWN TO LET
A NATIONAL TREND GO
BY UNNOTICED, PICK
UP ON BARBECUE.
KRAFT INTRODUCES
ITS FIRST BOTTLED
BARBECUE SAUCE IN
1960. Kraft

New Kraft Barbecue Sauce simmers real cook-out flavor right into the meat!

When it starts to simmer, the flavor really speaks up. This is the barbecue sauce that gives you the flavor you cook outdoors to get. The Kraft cooks made it that way—with nineteen herbs and spices. And once it's on the fire, those simmering spice flavors seep right in and keep the meat juicy. Try new Kraft Barbecue Sauce in your kitchen, too; cooks who do say that it brings its real cook-out flavor right indoors—and what could be better than that?

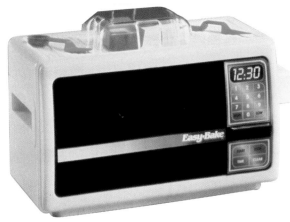

Relax.
Nothing could be more foolproof than Cool Whip? You don't have to beat it or mix it or mess with it. It comes already whipped, ready to serve. And the creamy, delicious taste never varies. It even has less calories than whipped cream you have to make. So spoon out the Cool Whip. And relax.

Don't blow your topping.

ABOVE: THE EASY-BAKE OVEN, NOW MANUFACTURED BY HASBRO, LOOKS MORE LIKE A MICROWAVE THAN ITS GREAT-GRANDMOTHER, WHICH WAS FASHIONABLE-1960S TURQUOISE. THE TIMER IS NOW DIGITAL. THIS MODEL RETAILS FOR $19.99— ONLY $4 MORE THAN THE 1963 ORIGINAL MODEL. Hasbro

ABOVE: COOL WHIP NONDAIRY TOPPING IS ROLLED OUT NATIONALLY IN 1967. COOL WHIP AND JELL-O BECOME AN ALL-AMERICAN DESSERT COMBINATION. Kraft

ABOVE: ELLA HELFRICH
DOESN'T TAKE HOME THE
GOLD IN THE 1966
PILLSBURY BAKE-OFF,
BUT HER TUNNEL OF
FUDGE CAKE IS THE
RECIPE THAT CATCHES THE
PUBLIC'S ATTENTION.
Pillsbury Bake-Off

ABOVE: BABY HORTON CRAWLS ALONG IN
COMMERCIALS ASSERTING THAT
"R-R-RUFFLES HAVE R-R-RIDGES." THE
PERFECT COMPANION OF SNACK-CRAZY,
DIP-LOVING AMERICAN NOSHERS, THE
RUFFLES BRAND IS ONE OF FIVE FRITO-LAY
PRODUCTS THAT GENERATES MORE THAN
$1 BILLION IN ANNUAL SALES. Frito-Lay

ABOVE: TASTER'S CHOICE FREEZE-DRIED
COFFEE IS INTRODUCED TO THE NATION'S
TABLES IN 1966. Nestle

Now Dad's an expert at "fryin' up" a chicken dinner!

Dad's night to cook is only one of so many special occasions when a delicious Swanson TV Brand Dinner answers your problems. It's just as handy when the teen-agers take over on a weekend, or when Mom's tired from shopping with the youngsters. It's all cooked, frozen, and ready to heat in its own individual serving tray—without thawing. So there's no work before—no dishes after. But how good it tastes—Swanson's extra-meaty, extra-tender golden-fried chicken with garden-fresh mixed vegetables and fluffy mashed potatoes. Don't wait—have some tonight.

Only Swanson has the secret of these delicious well-balanced TV Brand Dinners.

Swanson
TV. BRAND DINNERS

Also try Swanson TV Brand Turkey and Beef Dinners

MADE ONLY BY C. A. SWANSON & SONS, A SUBSIDIARY OF CAMPBELL SOUP COMPANY

LEFT: EVEN HAPLESS DAD CAN HEAT A TV DINNER. Swanson

Which Tony has the *Kellogg's* SUGAR FROSTED FLAKES?

TONY, SR.

TONY, JR.

They're both lucky tigers! Tony Sr. snacked his up right out of the box. Tony Jr. has his in a bowl with milk! Either way, you know these days 'most everybody has Kellogg's Sugar Frosted Flakes—Tonys, Smiths and folks with your name. Aren't they gr-r-reat fun to eat?

Kellogg's SUGAR FROSTED FLAKES

ABOVE: KELLOGG'S DRESSES UP ITS CORN FLAKES AND INTRODUCES KELLOGG'S FROSTED FLAKES IN THE 1950S. BUT THE CHARACTER WHO REPRESENTS THE CEREAL CHANGES OVER THE YEARS. THE FIRST MASCOT IS A KANGEROO, BUT LATER IS CHANGED TO TONY JR. AND FINALLY, TONY, HIS OWN GRAND 6 FOOT 6 INCH SELF. Kellogg's

RIGHT: EVEN KITCHEN APPLIANCES ARE MELLOW YELLOW IN THE 1960S. Maytag

BUFFALO WINGS

[S E R V E S   1 0 – 1 2]

36–40 chicken wing drumettes

Vegetable oil, for frying

1 stick butter

2-ounce bottle hot sauce

1 tablespoon vinegar

Blue-cheese salad dressing

Celery sticks

FRY CHICKEN pieces in about 2 inches of vegetable oil until done. Drain on paper towels. Meanwhile, melt butter in microwave or in small saucepan on top of stove. Add the entire bottle of hot sauce and the vinegar.

Remove hot wings to large platter, preferably one with a decent-size lip. Pour butter sauce over all and toss once. Serve with salad dressing and celery sticks on the side, along with plenty of napkins.

ABOVE: A BIT OF AMERICA IS FOUND IN VIETNAM. SOLDIERS HERALD THEIR HARD-WORKING MAYTAG WASHER IN A PHOTO FOR THE FOLKS BACK HOME. Maytag

Frito-Lay

Frito-Lay

LEFT: THE SOCIAL UPHEAVAL AND IRREVERENCE OF THE 1960S IS
REFLECTED IN THIS CLASSIC AD FOR LEVY'S BREAD. Library of Congress

WILTED SPINACH SALAD

[SERVES 2]

1 bunch spinach
Cooking oil
2 slices bacon, semi-cooked
¼ cup wine vinegar
½ cup olive oil
1 teaspoon Worcestershire sauce
Salt and pepper
1 hard-boiled egg, chopped

WASH AND drain spinach thoroughly. Cut bacon into 1-inch pieces and place in frying pan with small amount of oil. Cook until bacon is crisp. Add vinegar, oil, Worcestershire sauce, salt and pepper. Then pour dressing over spinach and mix thoroughly. (Mixture must be piping hot to wilt the spinach and give it a tender texture.) Place in individual salad bowls and sprinkle with chopped egg.

— *Saucepans & The Single Girl* by Jinx Fragen and
Judy Perry (Doubleday, 1965)

The Coca-Cola Company

LOVERLY CHICKEN

[S E R V E S   2]

3-pound chicken, cut into pieces

5 tablespoons butter, divided

1 tablespoon vegetable oil

Salt and pepper

Pinch of grated nutmeg

2 cups half-and-half cream

12 large mushroom caps

½ cup brandy

PULL ALL fat from body cavity of chicken and melt it in frying pan large enough to hold chicken pieces. Add 1 tablespoon butter and the oil. Brown chicken pieces on all sides, adding a little more butter and oil if necessary to get a good rich color. This will take about 20 minutes.

Now put chicken pieces in a serving casserole and season lightly with salt, freshly ground pepper and nutmeg. Set this aside for a moment while you heat the cream in the same frying pan. Stir well to pick up all the browned good-bits on the bottom.

Pour cream over chicken pieces and put casserole, uncovered, into a 350-degree oven. Bake for 1 hour.

While chicken cooks, wash mushroom caps (save the stems for tomorrow). Put 1 teaspoon of remaining butter in hollow of each cap.

When the hour is up and your chicken is done, take out of oven and distribute mushroom caps over it, butter side up. Turn oven up to broil or heat broiler if yours is separate. Slide casserole under broiler and cook mushrooms for about 5 minutes. Take casserole out and pour brandy over chicken; give it a quick stir to blend brandy with sauce in casserole and serve. Fluffy white rice and a pretty vegetable complete this dear little dinner.

— Helen Gurley Brown's *Single Girl's Cookbook* (Fawcett, 1969)

THE FIRST THROUGH-THE-DOOR WATER AND ICE DISPENSER WAS INTRODUCED IN 1969. THE MANUFACTURER POINTS OUT THAT THIS MAKES GETTING ICE SO SIMPLE EVEN A MAN CAN MANAGE. General Electric

1960–1969 TIMELINE

1960: The FDA approves birth-control pills.

1960: CBS profiles the plight of migrant farmworkers in California.

1960: About 35 percent of all women work outside the home, and they average 60 cents for every dollar earned by men.

1960: In a salute to modernism, appliance design becomes dominated by the "white cube" aesthetic, from stoves to washers and dryers.

1960: Reynolds Wrap Foil comes up with "Oven Tempered for Flexible Strength," a slogan that is used until 1972.

1960: Single-serve packages of ketchup are introduced.

1960: Aluminum cans are used for foods and beverages.

1960: The civil rights movement begins with lunch-counter sit-ins in Greensboro, N.C.

1960: Hereford, Texas, farmer Frank Ford founds Arrowhead Mills. He avoids using synthetic fertilizers, herbicides, and pesticides.

1961: The seminal *Mastering The Art of French Cooking* by Julia Child, Simone Beck, and Louisette Bertholle is published.

1961: Coffee-Mate is introduced.

1961: Sprite hits the market.

1962: John Glenn says that his first meal in space, applesauce through a tube, is nothing to write home about.

1962: Attorney General Robert Kennedy contacts the Grocery Manufacturers of America, asking for $12 million in food to ransom the Bay of Pigs soldiers held in Cuban jails. Gerber gives $920,000 in baby food; H.J. Heinz gives $1 million, and General Mills donates $500,000 in food. On December 29, President and Mrs. Kennedy welcome the prisoners home at the Orange Bowl in Miami.

1962: *Stalking the Wild Asparagus* by Euell Gibbons, 51, is published. Gibbons promotes nutrition through wild foods.

1962: Frozen pie crust is introduced.

1962: Handi Wrap is introduced.

1962: Rachel Carson writes *Silent Spring*, the first shot in the war against environmental pollution, particularly DDT.

1962: Gordon and Carole Segal renovate a 1,700-square-foot space in an old elevator factory in Chicago's Old Town. On a limited budget and with a staff of three, they outfit the location with crate lumber on the walls and arrange inventory with the shipping crates and barrels. The store offers gourmet cookware and contemporary housewares. By the end of the century, Crate and Barrel grows to 1,800 stores.

1962: Artist Andy Warhol exhibits "32 Campbell Soup Cans" in Los Angeles.

1962: The pull-tab can lid is patented.

1963: The 100th location of Dunkin' Donuts opens.

1963: General Electric introduces the first self-cleaning oven, the P-7. GE engineers are granted about 100 patents in developing the product.

1963: Bert Lahr, the Cowardly Lion in the "Wizard of Oz," introduces the "Betcha Can't Eat Just One" slogan in Lays Potato Chip TV ads.

1963: Queens, N.Y., homemaker Jean Nidetch, 39, founds Weight Watchers after losing 71 pounds. In 1978 Heinz acquires the company.

1963: Julia Child's "The French Chef" airs on WGBH-TV in Boston.

1963: Kenner develops the Easy-Bake Oven "toy." The "working" oven is introduced at the 1964 toy fair and more than 500,000 are sold the first year. The retail price is $15.99.

1964: Pop-Tarts are introduced.

1964: The Food Stamp Act is introduced as part of Lyndon B. Johnson's Great Society program. By 1982,

© Paul Child

$109.2 billion worth of stamps will be issued. In 1994, 10 percent of the population will receive food stamps, costing $24 billion a year.

1964: Colonel Sanders, 74, sells his Kentucky Fried Chicken idea for $2 million.

1964: Mr. Whipple begins squeezing Charmin.

1964: Buffalo wings are invented at the Anchor Bar in Buffalo, N.Y.

1964: The New York World's Fair introduces Americans to a smorgasbord of international fare with its 112 restaurants. Americans tuck into Belgian waffles—a treat that becomes a breakfast staple.

1964: Plastic is making life easier on the home front. Handi Food Bags, Handi Trash Bags, and Glad Trash Bags are rolled out.

1964: Cold duck pops up on the beverage scene.

1964: The first Coke in a can appears.

1965: "R-R-Ruffles Have Ridges" advertising campaign begins with Horton the Baby reaching for a bag of Ruffles Potato Chips.

1965: Pillsbury introduces Poppin' Fresh, the Pillsbury Doughboy, via a commercial for the company's ready-to-bake crescent rolls.

1965: "Happiness is . . . finding two olives in your martini when you're hungry," writes Johnny Carson in *Happiness Is a Dry Martini* (Doubleday, 1965).

1965: Dr. Robert Cade at the University of Florida develops a drink to help athletes replenish fluids and minerals. In 1967 the National Football League names Gatorade its official drink.

1965: Shake 'n' Bake is introduced.

1965: Tang is part of the cargo on Gemini 4. During the next decade, Tang is supplied on all manned Gemini and Apollo space flights. Into the millennium, Tang goes on all manned space missions.

1965: The Immigration Act of 1965 begins the influx of millions of people from China, Hong Kong, Taiwan, Japan, Korea, Thailand, Eastern Europe, the Philippines, India, the Middle East, Africa, Mexico, and Central and South America.

1965: Cool Whip is introduced and the following year is the sponsor of the No. 3-rated TV program, *The Andy Griffith Show.*

1966: Robert Mondavi Winery is founded.

1966: The Tunnel of Fudge cake, which wins second prize in the 17th Pillsbury Bake-Off for Ella Helfrich of Houston, is so popular that sales of bundt pans skyrocket. At the time, only one company, Northland Aluminum Products in Minneapolis, Minn., makes bundt pans and the factory has to go on a 24-hour production schedule to keep up with demand.

1966: Doritos, the first tortilla chips, are launched nationally.

1966: Catholics are permitted to eat meat on Friday.

1966: Bac*Os are introduced.

1966: Plastic bags on a roll for produce are introduced in grocery stores.

1966: Betty Friedan founds the National Organization for Women.

1966: Nabisco invents Easy Cheese Pasteurized Process Cheese Spread, also known as Snack Mate Processed Cheese Spread, cheese in an aerosol can.

1966: Instant Oatmeal is introduced.

1967: McCormick adds Beef Stroganoff Sauce Mix to its dehydrated sauce offerings.

1967: Campbell Soup Co. acquires Godiva Chocolate and begins supplying the U.S. from its Reading, Pa., plant.

1967: Lawry's Taco Seasoning is introduced.

1967: It's no longer simply the rich who make the pilgrimage to Europe. As air travel becomes more affordable, the middle class gets a taste of different, and sometimes finer, cuisine.

1967: Gatorade is introduced.

1969: Pringles potato chips are introduced.

1969: Dave Thomas opens the first Wendy's in Columbus, Ohio. He has already made $1 million by taking over Kentucky Fried Chicken restaurants and making them profitable. Wendy's is named for his daughter.

1969: The first Cracker Barrel Old Country Store opens along Interstate 40 in Lebanon, Tenn. In 1977, because of the oil embargo, the 13-store company decides to stop selling gasoline. By 1999 the company has 500 stores along America's interstates.

1970–1979

Single was sexy in the 1970s. Perhaps in response to the politically and socially tumultuous 1960s, the 1970s were all about "me."

A war in Vietnam tore this country apart by the time it was finally over and lost in middecade. President Nixon was ousted from his job, throwing the country into further disarray.

Felix and Oscar showed us that it was all right, though often loony, to be divorced. The Bradys portrayed families that were reconstructed and blended. Mary Richards proved that living la dolce sola could be a hat-flinging good time.

T.G.I. Friday's had 10 locations by 1975, popular spots for singles sipping the likes of fuzzy navels and tequila sunrises as they noshed on potato skins. Friday's, and its copycats, were often decorated with a plethora of well-displayed junk and hanging plants, leading to the term "fern bars."

Further liberated by the feminist movement, women who chose to work outside the home as well as raise children, had help from food producers always willing to make things easier. Breakfast could now be purchased at McDonald's, and food processors became a part of the home kitchen.

While ethnic foods were no longer relegated to the coasts, where most immigrants landed, Americans were far from the familiarity with foreign food that they were to reach by the end of the century. There were Taco Bell locations in tiny towns in Missouri, but President Ford still did not know to remove the corn husk from a tamale before eating it.

And as always, the American diet continued to fuel debate.

The beliefs espoused on communes and by hippies of the 1960s moved into the country's culinary mainstream.

Deborah Madison was one of a group of American Zen Buddhists who opened the acclaimed Greens vegetarian restaurant in San Francisco in 1979. Quaker Oats introduced granola to the mainstream supermarket in 1972. Yogurt was no longer relegated to Greek and Middle Eastern enclaves.

And low-fat became big business, as the extreme thinness that was so chic in the 1960s continued to be considered the height of beauty. The weight-loss method of choice across college campuses of the time was Dr. Stillman's eight glasses of water//boiled eggs//cheese//meat diet. The diet would be a huge fad again— at the end of the century when those college kids hit the wall of middle age.

You make it with hot water because **we made it with milk.** Natural B-vitamins, protein and minerals of nonfat dry milk are already in Carnation's own rich cocoa formula. So all you do

ABOVE: CARNATION'S HOT CHOCOLATE MIX DEBUTS IN 1972. Nestle

LEFT: McDONALD'S ROLLS OUT ITS EGG McMUFFIN, THE NATION'S FIRST FAST-FOOD RESTAURANT BREAKFAST ITEM, IN 1973. McDonald's Corp.

TOP LEFT: WITH MORE AND MORE WOMEN WORKING OUTSIDE THE HOME, DINNER FROM A JAR BECOMES COMMONPLACE IN THE 1970s. Lipton

QUICHE LORRAINE

[Serves 8]

6 slices bacon, chopped

½ cup onion, chopped

1½ cups (6 ounces) shredded Swiss cheese

Unbaked 9-inch deep-dish pastry pie shell

1½ cups (12-ounce can) evaporated milk

3 large eggs, well beaten

¼ teaspoon salt

⅛ teaspoon ground black pepper

⅛ teaspoon ground nutmeg

Preheat oven to 350 degrees.
Cook bacon in large skillet over medium heat. When bacon starts to turn brown, add onion.
Cook until bacon is crisp; drain. Sprinkle cheese into bottom of pie shell. Top with bacon mixture.
Combine evaporated milk, eggs, salt, pepper, and nutmeg in small bowl until blended. Pour into pie shell.
Bake for 30 to 35 minutes or until knife inserted halfway between center and edge comes out clean.
Cool for 5 minutes on wire rack before serving.

— Nestle

ABOVE: THE POLITICAL ACTIVISM OF THE 1960S CONTINUED INTO THE 1970S. CONSUMERS PROTESTED THE LIVING CONDITIONS AND WAGES OF MIGRANT FARM WORKERS BY BOYCOTTING GRAPES AND LETTUCE—TWO AGRICULTURAL PRODUCTS WHERE MANUAL LABOR WAS KEY TO HARVEST. Library of Congress

MENU
CHEZ PANISSE CAFE

MONDAY LUNCH · AUGUST 1, 1988

Tomato soup with crème fraîche, $4.50

Figs, mango, pickled cherries, and prosciutto, $7.50

Baked Sonoma goat cheese with garden lettuce salad, $7.50

Garden lettuce salad, $6.00

·

Pizza with roasted peppers, capers, and olives,
large, $12.50; small, $7.50

Calzone with goat cheese, mozzarella, prosciutto, and garlic, $11.00

·

Grilled chicken salad with green beans, shell beans, egg,
tomatoes, anchovies, and aioli toast, $9.75

Steamed salmon with cucumbers, beurre blanc, and chervil, $11.50

Mixed grill with cured pork, squash, eggplant, and tomatoes, $10.50

Pasta with potatoes and pesto, $9.50

·

*Pistachio torte with orange crème anglaise, $5.00

Rhubarb crisp with vanilla ice cream, $5.50

Peaches with red and golden raspberries, $4.75

Chocolate almond ice cream, $4.50

*while available

Most of our produce is organically grown; an increasing proportion of our meat
is from animals raised in a wholesome way, without chemical additives.

We serve lunch from 11:30 AM until 3:00 PM, Monday through Friday, and
until 4:30 PM on Saturday; from 3:00 to 5:00, salads and desserts are
served at the bar. For lunch reservations, call 548-5049 the same day.

Menu

CHEZ PANISSE CAFÉ · LUNCH MENU FOR DECEMBER 1, 1987
THE THIRTEENTH ANNUAL NEW ZINFANDEL FESTIVAL

* Red wine and red onion soup with Gruyère, $4.00

* Goose and pork terrine with curly endive and beets, $6.50

Leeks vinaigrette with chervil and hard cooked egg, $6.00

Antipasto plate: stuffed prosciutto, eggplant croûton,
roasted peppers, and anchovies, $7.50

* Garden lettuce salad, $5.00

Pizza with fontina, mozzarella, Gorgonzola, walnuts, and chervil,
small, $6.50 · large, $11.50

Calzone with garden salad, $8.00

Mussels steamed in red wine with grilled garlic toast, $8.50

Red pepper fettuccine with sausage,
flat black cabbage, and herbs, $9.50

Eggplant stew with toast, $7.50

·

Persimmon pudding, $4.50

Key lime pie, $4.50

Oranges and pomegranates in caramel syrup, $4.00

·

New Zinfandel from Joseph Phelps: glass, $2.00 · bottle, $8.00

* Also available at the bar between three and five PM.

Chez Panisse Restaurant
15% service may be charged to parties of six or more.
The café is open late for dinner—untill 11:30 PM
Lunch : Monday–Friday, 11:30 AM – 3:00 PM;
Saturday, 11:30 AM – 4:30 PM
Dinner: Monday–Saturday, 5:00 PM – 11:30 PM

ABOVE AND RIGHT: ALICE WATERS
OPENS CHEZ PANISSE IN BERKELEY,
CALIF., IN 1971. WATERS' VISION OF
USING ONLY FRESH, LOCALLY GROWN
INGREDIENTS GIVES BIRTH TO NEW
CALIFORNIA CUISINE AND TO THE
GROWTH IN RESTAURANT INNOVATIONS
NEVER BEFORE SEEN IN THIS COUNTRY.
City of Los Angeles Public Library

LEFT: THE HORNBACHER
FAMILY OF STORY CITY,
IOWA, IN 1974 TAKES TOP
HONORS BY OWNING THE
OLDEST AUTOMATIC
MAYTAG WASHER. THIS
WASHER IS 12TH OFF THE
ASSEMBLY LINE IN BUSY
1949. Maytag

ABOVE AND BELOW: MIKEY, GOADED INTO EATING NEW LIFE CEREAL BY HIS TWO BROTHERS, BECOMES ONE OF THE MOST BELOVED CHARACTERS IN A COMMERCIAL. General Mills

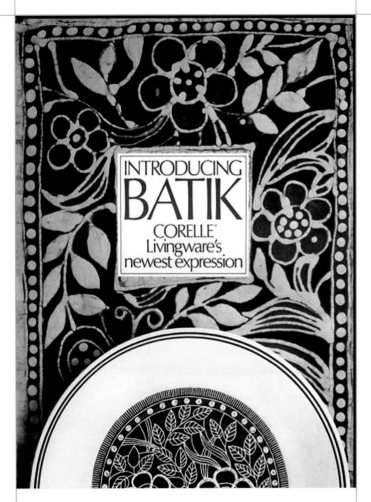

ABOVE: AMERICA'S FAVORITE NONBREAKABLE DINNERWARE GETS WITH IT IN 1977.

The working woman's household wrap.

It's strong all over, for freezer-to-oven cooking.

One thing a busy woman needs (and never gets enough of) is time. So Reynolds Wrap created new freezer-to-oven cooking just for you.

The basic idea is beautiful . . . foil-wrapped frozen meats, poultry and fish go right from the freezer into the oven, without thawing. It saves time, and everything you cook comes out tender and flavorful because you don't lose the juices, as you do when you thaw. It's all done with Heavy Duty Reynolds Wrap, oven-tempered for flexible strength to resist tearing.

No-thaw roast. Delicious and juicy.

1. Remove foil-wrapped meat from freezer and place in foil-lined roasting pan. Preheat oven to 400°. Loosen foil across top and ends of meat to allow heat to circulate.
2. For a 4 lb. roast, allow 45 min. per lb. for rare, 52 min. per lb. for medium, up to 60 minutes per lb. for well-done.
3. During final half-hour of roasting, turn foil back from meat completely so roast can brown. Insert meat thermometer for desired degree of doneness. Meat comes out beautifully brown, actually tastier than if you'd thawed it.

No-thaw poultry. Tender and moist.

1. Place frozen foil wrapped bird in foil-lined roasting pan. Preheat oven to 450°. Loosen foil across top and at ends to allow heat to circulate.
2. Roasting time:
8½ to 4 lb. chicken . . . 2 hrs, 20 min.
4½ to 5 lb. bird . . . 2 hrs, 50 min.
5½ to 6 lb. bird . . . 3 hrs, 45 min.
3. For final 20 minutes, turn foil back from bird, baste for browning.

Elegant freeze-and-serve English Trifle.

Line a bowl or a mold with Heavy Duty Reynolds Wrap. Layer as follows . . . a layer of lady fingers sprinkled with sherry, raspberry jam, vanilla pudding. Continue layering until bowl is filled. Cover tightly with foil and freeze. When ready to serve, remove foil from top of dessert, invert on platter. Remove bowl, strip off foil, garnish with whipped topping and candied fruit.

Start right. Wrap it right.

Food experts agree . . . heavy duty aluminum foil is best for freezing. So remove the plastic wrap food comes in. This wrap is fine for display in the meat counters, but was not made for freezing.

Place food in center of large sheet of Heavy Duty Reynolds Wrap. Bring foil up over top of food and double-fold, pressing down tightly to remove air. Frigid air can cause food to dry out and lose flavor. Reynolds Wrap keeps air out, moisture in. After you fold ends up tight against food, label package with contents and date. Freeze.

Reynolds Wrap. Strong all over. Count on it.

ReynoldsWrap HEAVY DUTY
Aluminum Foil
37¢ SQ. FT.
Oven-tempered for flexible strength.

March 1973

Swansons

PLAYBOY PAELLA

[SERVES 6-8]

1½ pounds pork loin, center cut

4 chicken breasts, boned and skinned

1 pound sliced leg of veal, pounded thin, as for scallopini

¼ pound chicken livers

1 pound raw shrimp

1 pound fresh peas or 10-ounce package frozen peas

1 cup oil, divided

½ pound chorizo, cut into ¼-inch slices

2 sweet red peppers or canned pimentos

2 green bell peppers

¼ pound fresh mushrooms, thinly sliced

3 large cloves garlic

1 large Spanish onion, minced extremely fine

¼ teaspoon saffron powder

½ teaspoon oregano

2 cups long-grain rice

4 to 5 cups chicken broth, canned or fresh

½ pound bay scallops

Salt and pepper

REMOVE BONE and fat from pork. Cut into 1-inch squares, ¼ inch thick. Cut chicken crosswise into 1-inch chunks. Cube veal into 1-inch squares. Cut chicken liver pairs into halves. Cut peppers into ½-inch squares, discarding stem ends, seeds, and membranes. Using scissors, cut shrimp shells through back and underside, leaving shells on shrimp and tails intact. Shell fresh peas and set aside. Heat ½ cup oil in paella pan. Sauté pork until deep brown; remove from pan. Sauté chicken, chorizo, veal, and chicken livers until light brown; remove from pan. Sauté peppers and mushrooms until just barely tender, adding more oil to pan if necessary; remove from pan. Wash and dry pan.

Add ½ cup oil and heat over flames. Add garlic, onion, saffron, oregano and rice and stir well. Sauté, stirring constantly, 5 minutes. Add chicken broth, pork, chicken, chorizo, veal, chicken livers, scallops, peppers, mushrooms, and shrimp.

Bring liquid to boil. If chicken broth is unseasoned, add 1 to 2 teaspoons salt. Reduce heat; simmer 10 minutes. Add peas and simmer 15–25 minutes longer, stirring gently but as little as possible, to keep ingredients from sticking to pan bottom. Sprinkle with salt and pepper.

— *Playboy's International Gourmet* by Thomas Mario (Playboy Press, 1971)

SPINACH 'N' RADISH SALAD

[SERVES 8]

6 cups fresh spinach
1 ½ cups sliced radishes
1 cup sliced onion
¼ cup Tomato Ketchup Salad Dressing (see below)

COMBINE SPINACH, radishes and onion until well mixed. Toss with salad dressing.

———————

TOMATO KETCHUP
SALAD DRESSING

[YIELDS 2 CUPS]

1 cup vegetable oil
⅓ cup vinegar
½ cup ketchup
¼ cup sugar
2 teaspoons dry mustard
1 teaspoon salt
1 teaspoon Worcestershire sauce
½ teaspoon pepper

MEASURE INGREDIENTS into blender; cover. Blend at high speed about 1 minute. Serve over salad.

— *Dietary Control of Cholesterol* (Fleischmann's Margarine, 1972)

1970: Orville Redenbacher's Gourmet Popping Corn is introduced. Agronomist Redenbacher finds a yellow corn that expands nearly twice as much as other brands. In five years, it is the country's largest-selling brand.

1970: Hamburger Helper is introduced.

1970: The first overseas Dunkin' Donuts opens in Japan.

1970: Fifteen percent of flour sold in the United States is sold to home consumers.

1970: Resealable plastic bags and Reynolds Oven Bags are introduced.

1970: Morton introduces Salt Substitute and, in 1973, brings out Lite Salt.

1971: The nation's first salad bar is laid out at R.J. Grunts, a singles bar and restaurant in Chicago.

1971: Rival trademarks the Crock-Pot.

1971: McDonald's opens in Tokyo, its first international site.

1971: Alice Waters opens Chez Panisse in Berkeley, Calif. A three-course meal costs less than $8.

1971: Starbucks is founded at Pike Place Market in Seattle. The company goes public in 1992.

1971: McCormick introduces its Roast in Bag, a "kit" to make baking easier. Each package is outfitted with seasonings and a bag for holding all the ingredients. All the cook adds is the fresh ingredients—meat and vegetables. The first three varieties are Savory Oven

ABOVE: ALTHOUGH FAST-FOOD RESTAU-RANTS ARE SPROUTING THROUGHOT THE COUNTRY IN THE 1970s, LOCAL FAVORITES CONTINUE. THIS TEXAS BARBECUE JOINT IS AS MUCH A FIXTURE OF THE LANDSCAPE AS IS THE OIL DERRICK BESIDE IT. Library of Congress

Roasting Bag for chicken, Pot Roast, and Spareribs. Later the product is renamed Bag 'n Season.

1972: Celestial Seasonings Herbal Teas are introduced.

1972: "He likes it! Hey Mikey!" Two older brothers get Mikey to try the family's new cereal, Life, and he likes it. The popular television commercial runs for 12 years. The brothers portrayed in the commercial are in fact, really brothers: Tom and Michael Gilchrist plus John Gilchrist as Mikey.

1972: Snapple fruit juices are introduced.

1972: The New York State Division of Human Rights prohibits ladies' nights at Yankee Stadium because they discriminate against men.

1972: Quaker Oats 100% Natural, the first granola for the masses, is introduced.

1972: Tootsie Roll acquires two famous candy names, Mason Dots and Crows.

1972: Ziploc Storage Bags are introduced.

1973: The Clorox Corp. buys the rights to Hidden Valley dressing from Steve Henson, who began serving his concoction at his dude ranch near Santa Barbara in 1954.

1973: "Eating Well Is the Best Revenge" is the October issue of *New York* magazine. America is becoming familiar with the wide world of cuisine.

1973: Tupperware sees demographic changes and begins serving those markets. One introduction is the Instant Seal, an easier-to-open container designed for seniors. As more marriages end in divorce, Tupperware sees its sales ranks swell with women who need to work around the schedules of their children.

1973: McDonald's introduces the Egg McMuffin, the first fast-food breakfast item.

1973: Cup O'Noodles is introduced.

1973: Moosewood, a vegetarian collective restaurant, opens in Ithaca, N.Y.

1973: Carl Sontheimer introduces the Cuisinart Food Processor at the National Housewares Exposition in Chicago. Buyers at first are cool to the $140 machine, but Julia Child's and James Beard's praise garner a favorable reaction. The product becomes so hot during the 1976 Christmas season that retailers sell empty boxes as promises for future delivery.

1973: Stove Top Stuffing is introduced.

1973: Rising food costs, and shortages of some meat cuts, lead many Americans into the kitchen to try recipes beyond casseroles.

1974: The first product printed with a UPC (Universal Product Code)—a 10-pack of Juicy Fruit Gum—is scanned at March Supermarket in Troy, Ohio. An IBM engineer is credited with the patent, although several companies are working on the project at the request of a group of grocery stores.

1974: Vincent Marotta and Samuel Glazer gain nationwide recognition for their Mr. Coffee (invented in 1972) by signing Joe DiMaggio as their spokesman.

1974: Yoplait yogurt, Miller Lite (the first light beer), and Mrs. Field's Cookies are introduced.

WHEN INTRODUCED, THE EXPENSIVE FOOD PROCESSOR WAS VIEWED AS AN INDULGENCE. IT SOON BECAME MANDATORY EQUIPMENT FOR ANYONE WHO CONSIDERED THEMSELVES A GOOD COOK. Conair Corp.

1975: The word *fajita* appears in print for the first time. From the Spanish faja, "girdle" or "strip," the word actually means the cut of meat itself. Cooking the meat over wood has always been a Texas tradition, but how the name derived is anyone's guess, including that of Homero Recio, who in 1984 used a fellowship to Texas A&M to study the subject. But Texas restaurants should probably thank Ninfa Laurenzo for popularizing the item because she put it on her menu at the original Ninfa's in Houston, Texas, in 1973 as tacos *al carbon*.

1975: American consumption of soft drinks surpasses that of coffee.

1975: The ballpark nacho is born at the Texas Rangers' Arlington Stadium.

1975: Famous Amos Chocolate Chip Cookies are introduced.

1975: Country Time powdered lemonade is introduced to regional markets. In 1984 the product is launched nationally.

1976: Tom Wolfe calls the 1970s the "Me Decade," and Burger King follows with the "Have It Your Way" campaign.

1977: Reynolds Freezer Paper is introduced.

1977: Plastic soda bottles are first recycled.

The PET (polyethylene-terephthalate) bottle is invented by Nathaniel Wyeth (brother of artist Andrew and son of artist-illustrator Newel Convers [N.C.] Wyeth). Trained as an engineer, Wyeth works for DuPont Corp.

In 1967 he starts working on the project for which pop culture will most remember him. Carbonated beverage could not be bottled in plastic because the containers would explode. Wyeth develops a stronger system of molding the plastic, enabling the company to produce a bottle that is light, clear and resilient. He patents the process in 1973. By the end of the century, PET products are one of the most recycled products in the country. The no. 1 plastic is most often used as fiberfill or as a synthetic fabric. About 50 percent of polyester carpet made in America uses recycled PET bottles.

1977: The term "comfort food" first appears in print in the *Washington Post Magazine*. The author uses the term in reference to grits, but by the 1980s the term has grown to mean, in many ways, the food of childhood and encompasses everyday dishes such as meatloaf, mashed potatoes, macaroni and cheese, and gelatin desserts.

1977: The plastic grocery bag is introduced to the supermarket industry.

1977: Dean & DeLuca and The Silver Palate specialty-food stores open in New York City.

1978: General Electric offers the first over-the-range microwave oven: the SpaceMaker.

1978: For the first time, more women than men enter college.

1978: McCormick introduces its first low-fat product: Lite Gravy.

1978: Ben and Jerry's Homemade Ice Cream and Crepes opens in Vermont.

1979: Paul Prudhomme, formerly of Commander's Palace, opens K-Paul Louisiana Kitchen in New Orleans, and the Cajun craze is on.

1980–1989

WHAT ALICE WATERS wrought in Berkeley, Calif., in 1971 exploded across the country the following decade. Fueled by an economy that was ethically out of control, America was turning dining into theater.

The 1980s were chock-full of the likes of junk-bond kings Michael Milken and Ivan Boesky. John Z. DeLorean was acquitted on charges of smuggling cocaine to help his financially strapped automobile company. The Donald and Ivana Trump were living the high life in New York City. Across the way, Leona Helmsley was brow beating her staff. On the other coast, Zsa Zsa Gabor was slapping Beverly Hills' Finest.

Nancy Reagan's presence in the White House occasioned a new set of White House china and more formal entertaining than the barbecues of the Carter era.

The living was high, and there were lots of young chefs who were having no trouble finding backers for restaurants that would showcase the new American cuisine.

In Texas, modern southwestern food emerged from the work of Stephan Pyles, Dean Fearing, Robert Del Grande, and Anne Greer. Mark Miller, an alumnus of Chez Panisse, took his show to Santa Fe and opened the Coyote Cafe, updating New Mexico classics. Jasper White was working with New England ingredients in Boston.

The chefs were helped in their quest by a burgeoning group of boutique producers—from cheese makers to specialty vegetable farmers to operations like Texas' Broken Arrow Ranch, which raises game animals.

And it's not just at home that American food was getting raves. By 1988 McDonald's had established itself as one of France's most popular fast-food operators. Burger King opened a location in Dresden, East Germany, as the Berlin Wall came down.

ABOVE: 7-ELEVEN SUPER-SIZES BEVERAGES WITH THE 32-OUNCE BIG GULP. 7-Eleven

The stock market crash of 1987 took a lot of air out of the social balloon.

Good spirits were further dampened by American Medical Association recommendations that blood serum cholesterol levels shouldn't exceed 200 milligrams. Eggs were bad, fried foods were bad, caffeine was bad, beef was bad, butter was bad. Grocery stores nationwide experienced runs on oat bran by consumers pumping themselves full of fiber to flush cholesterol from their systems.

TOP RIGHT: INTRODUCED IN 1975, MILLER BREWING USES THE CATCHY "TASTES GREAT, LESS FILLING" IN ITS ADVERTISING. Miller Brewing Co.

RIGHT: *COOKING LIGHT* LAUNCHES IN 1987, SHOWCASING HEALTHFUL MEALS AND ACTIVE LIFESTYLES. IT BECOMES THE NATION'S BEST-SELLING FOOD MAGAZINE. Cooking Light Magazine

M&M's DOES NOT stand for Mars & Mars, although the candy that "melts in your mouth, not in your hand" is the brainchild of Forrest Mars. Mars gets the idea for the little candies while traveling through Spain in the 1930s. There, he sees soldiers on maneuvers eating sugar-crusted chocolates. Back in America, he takes his idea to the folks in Hershey, Pa.— well, to one man, actually.

William Murrie is the yin to Milton Hershey's yang—the consummate businessman who builds the infrastructure that makes Hershey the behemoth it remains a century later. Hershey is the innovator; Murrie was the navigator. And Murrie has

Mars, Inc.

grown sons, which cagey Forrest Mars knows. Mars proposes that Murrie's son, Bruce, become a partner with him in the candy business. They could name the little morsels "M&M's" for "Mars and Murrie."

It is a done deal.

What Mars doesn't say to Murrie père is that he knows war is on the horizon. He also knows that Hershey is the nation's largest chocolate producer. And through the Murrie in M&M's, Mars also has access to chocolate. And so, in 1941, the first M&M's are sold to the public after much assistance with Hershey in tooling the factory. The partnership, however, is not to last, and Mars eventually buys out Murrie's interest in the little candies that melt in your mouth, not in your hand.

Jolly little M&M's, however, carry on, celebrating their 50th birthday in 1991.

1941: M&M's Plain Chocolate Candies, packaged in cardboard tubes, are sold to the military as a convenient food that won't melt in any climate. The original colors are brown, yellow, orange, red, green, and violet. (Violet was later replaced by tan.)

1948: M&M's change to the brown package familiar to today's consumers.

1954: M&M's Peanut Chocolate Candies are introduced, in brown only. The company rolls out the "melts in your mouth, not in your hands" slogan. Mars is an innovator in marketing to parents via their children.

1960: Peanut M&M's add red, green, and yellow to their color mix.

1976: Orange is added to M&M's peanut mix. Mars also removes red M&M's from the plain candies. There is public controversy surrounding red dye, but not the one Mars uses. To avoid confusion, the company removes the red candies.

1987: Red M&M's return.

1995: Mars allows America to vote for a new color to be added to regular M&M's. The winner is blue with a big 54 percent.

Chocolate Goes to Hollywood

Steven Spielberg's "people" first approach Mars with a new sort of marketing idea. They have a movie in production about an alien and think it would be fun for the creature to be lured into his first earthly house with M&M candies. Mars passes, thinking the idea just a bit too otherworldly.

Hershey's isn't too excited, either. In fact, the business executive who meets with Spielberg's people pays for his own ticket to Los Angeles. However, Reese's Pieces, a relatively new product for the company, isn't doing great guns. Sales are flat.

On a gut feeling more than anything else (after all, Spielberg's most recent film was the underwhelmingly received 1941), a deal is inked for Hershey's to promote E.T. with $1 million in advertising. In return, Hershey's could use E.T. in its own ads.

Within two weeks of the movie's premiere, Reese's Pieces sales triple. And they are in every movie theater's concession stands.

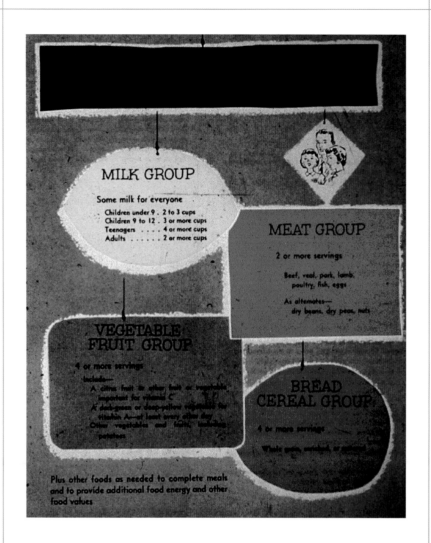

MILK GROUP

Some milk for everyone

Children under 9 . 2 to 3 cups
Children 9 to 12 . 3 or more cups
Teenagers . . . . 4 or more cups
Adults . . . . . . 2 or more cups

MEAT GROUP

2 or more servings

Beef, veal, pork, lamb,
poultry, fish, eggs

As alternates—
dry beans, dry peas, nuts

VEGETABLE
FRUIT GROUP

4 or more servings

Include—

A citrus fruit or other fruit or vegetable
important for vitamin C
A dark-green or deep-yellow vegetable for
vitamin A—at least every other day
Other vegetables and fruits, including
potatoes

BREAD
CEREAL GROUP

4 or more servings

Whole grain, enriched or restored

Plus other foods as needed to complete meals
and to provide additional food energy and other
food values

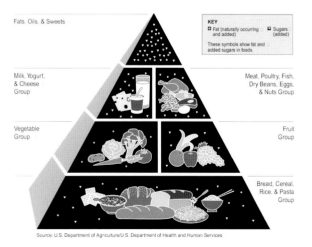

Fats, Oils, & Sweets

KEY
▣ Fat (naturally occurring ▼ Sugars
and added)   (added)
These symbols show fat and
added sugars in foods.

Milk, Yogurt,
& Cheese
Group

Meat, Poultry, Fish,
Dry Beans, Eggs,
& Nuts Group

Vegetable
Group

Fruit
Group

Bread, Cereal,
Rice, & Pasta
Group

Source: U.S. Department of Agriculture/U.S. Department of Health and Human Services

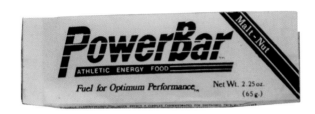

ABOVE: Olympic marathon runner Brian
Maxwell and his wife, Jennifer, a
competitive runner and nutritionist,
develop PowerBars in their Berkeley,
Calif., kitchen, which hit the market
in 1986. Power Bar

FITS THE BUN, BITE FOR BITE.™

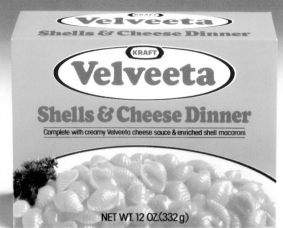

ABOVE: MACARONI AND CHEESE FOR GROWN-UPS IS INTRODUCED IN 1982. Kraft

ABOVE: A DOG HAS GOT TO MATCH ITS BUN. THESE BUN-LENGTH FRANKS APPEAR IN 1987. Kraft

ABOVE: McNUGGETS, DRIVE-THROUGH CHICKEN MINUS THE BONES, ARE A HIT RIGHT OUT OF THE BOX. McDonald's Corp.

CAESAR SALAD

[Yields 6 Servings]

1 or 2 coddled eggs, *see "Note"*

3 medium heads romaine lettuce

⅓ cup olive oil

2–3 Tbsp. wine vinegar

2 Tbsp. lemon juice

3 cloves garlic, crushed

Salt and pepper

4 to 5 dashes Worcestershire sauce

Freshly grated Parmesan cheese, divided

Croutons for garnish

NOTE: *To coddle eggs: bring 2 inches of water in small saucepan to a boil. Turn off heat. Using a slotted spoon, lower 1 to 2 eggs into water and let stand for one minute. Remove eggs and let cool.*

RINSE ROMAINE lettuce, drain well. Tear leaves into bite size pieces and place in a salad bowl. Drizzle over salad, olive oil, wine vinegar, and lemon juice. Break the coddled eggs over the center of salad. Crush garlic and sprinkle over salad. Season with salt and freshly ground pepper. Add Worcestershire sauce. Sprinkle with grated Parmesan cheese then lightly toss until ingredients are well combined. Garnish with croutons and additional grated cheese.

— Lea & Perrins

BACON, TOMATO AND PESTO PIZZA

[Serves 4]

1 Boboli pizza crust

½ cup prepared pesto

Sliced roma tomatoes

6 pieces bacon, cooked until limp, not crispy, torn into thirds

Mozzarella and Parmesan cheese

TOP PIZZA crust with the prepared pesto. Distribute tomatoes around the pizza and top with the bacon. Top with the mozzarella, then the Parmesan cheese. Bake at 420 degrees until the cheese is melted.

MOZZARELLA CO.'S CHICKEN BREASTS

[SERVES 4]

2 whole large chicken breasts, skinned, boned and halved (2 pounds, total)

Salt, to taste

Freshly ground black pepper, to taste

2 tablespoons unsalted butter

1 clove garlic

½ cup white wine

8 ounces fresh mozzarella, cut into ¼-inch slices

4 sprigs fresh tarragon

SEASON THE chicken breasts with salt and pepper. Melt butter in a large skillet over medium heat. Add garlic and chicken breasts and sauté for 6 to 10 minutes, or until golden brown on both sides, turning as necessary. Remove to a plate and keep warm. Deglaze the pan with the wine and simmer briefly to reduce to half its original volume. Return the chicken to the skillet and cook for 1 minute.

Place 2 slices of fresh mozzarella on top of each chicken breast and place 1 sprig of tarragon on top. Cover the pan and remove it from the heat. Set aside in a warm place for a few minutes and let the mozzarella just soften and begin to melt. Sprinkle with additional salt or pepper, as desired. Remove the garlic.

To serve, spoon some of the sauce over chicken breasts.

— Mozzarella Co., Dallas, Tex.

ABOVE: FIRST USED IN REFERRING TO BONELESS CHICKEN PIECES, "TENDERS" BECOMES A BUZZWORD IN FISH AND BEEF LINGO AS WELL. Gorton's Corp.

ABOVE: CHOCOLATE PUDDING GETS ON THE STICK IN 1980. Kraft

BACARDI DOUBLE-CHOCOLATE RUM CAKE

[SERVES 12–16]

18.5 ounce chocolate cake mix

1 package chocolate instant pudding

4 eggs

1 cup Bacardi Dark Rum, divided

¾ cup plus 1 teaspoon water, divided

½ cup vegetable oil

2 cups semisweet chocolate chips, divided

1 cup raspberry preserves

2 tablespoons shortening

1 ounce white chocolate

PREHEAT OVEN to 350 degrees. Combine cake mix, pudding, eggs, ½ cup rum, ¾ cup water, and oil in large mixing bowl. Using electric mixer, beat at low speed until moistened. Beat at medium speed 2 minutes. Stir in 1 cup chocolate chips. Pour batter into greased 12-cup bundt pan or 10-inch tube pan. Bake 50 to 60 minutes until cake tests done. Cool in pan 15 minutes. Remove from pan; cool on rack.

In a small saucepan, heat raspberry preserves and remaining ½ cup rum. Strain through sieve to remove seeds. Place cake on serving plate. Prick surface of cake with fork. Brush raspberry glaze evenly over cake, allowing cake to absorb glaze. Repeat until all glaze is absorbed.

In bowl, combine remaining 1 cup chocolate chips and shortening. Microwave on high 1 minute or until melted. Stir until smooth. Or, heat mixture over hot (not boiling) water until chocolate melts and mixture is smooth. Spoon chocolate icing over cake. Let stand 10 minutes. In small bowl, combine white chocolate and 1 teaspoon water. Microwave on high 30 seconds or until melted. Or, melt over hot (not boiling) water. Drizzle on top of chocolate icing.

— Bacardi recipe pamphlet

Americans play with their food in the 1980s—a la Wolfgang Puck and Paul Prudhomme—and New Coke comes and goes.

1980: McDonald's tests chicken McNuggets in Knoxville, Tenn., and gets such a huge response that its supplier can't keep up with demand.

1980: More than half of all women work outside the home. Thirty-two percent of white women and 25 percent of black women are employed as clerical workers. The numbers for Asian and Hispanic women fall somewhere in between.

1980: Blue Bell rolls out Cookies 'n Cream Ice Cream as a full-time year-around flavor. The first company to combine cookie crumbs and ice cream, the creamery in Bonham, Texas, has some trouble getting started. First, there isn't a supply of cookie crumbs. One employee is assigned the full-time job of ripping open truckloads of cookie bags and feeding the cookies into a crumbling machine. Another employee stirs the cookies and slowly adds them into the ice cream mix. By 1979 Blue Bell introduces the combination in grocery stores on a trial run.

1980: The decade sees a growth in farm-raised seafood, including mussels, crawfish, trout, oysters, catfish, salmon, striped bass, and tilapia.

1980: The Zagat Restaurant Survey publishes its first guide to New York City restaurants.

1980: Whole Food Market opens in Austin, Tex., with a staff of 19. By the end of the century, through growth and acquisition, the chain is the No. 1 natural-foods grocer in the U.S.

THE FIRST WHOLE FOODS AUSTIN STORE. Whole Foods

1980: 7-Eleven, the world's largest convenience store operation, introduces the 32-ounce Big Gulp. That soft drink serving size is so popular that, in 1987 the company brings out the Super Big Gulp, 44 ounces of sipping pleasure. And to further prove that bigger is better in America, in 1992 the chain introduces the 64-ounce Double Gulp. By comparison, the 1916 Coke bottle held 6.5 ounces.

1981: U.S. pasta consumption balloons—it's 13 pounds per person per year. In 1968 it was 6.2 pounds.

1981: Nestle, owner of Stouffer's Corp., rolls out Lean Cuisine.

1981: Americans spend 28 cents of every food dollar in a restaurant, fast-food store or take-home market, up from 26 cents in 1969.

1981: President Reagan stocks the White House with his favorite treat—jelly beans.

1982: Anheauser-Busch introduces Bud Light.

1982: Chosen by astronauts, M&M's become the first chocolate candies in space.

ABOVE: THIS CEREAL AIMED AT AN AGING POPULATION APPEARS IN 1982. Kraft

1982: Tupperware gets into the busy swim of the decade with Reheatables and the TupperWave line; the first is designed for warming leftovers, the second for frozen foods. A Microsteamer is added to the line: quick cooking for two.

1982: Campbell Soup introduces Swanson Great Starts frozen breakfast.

1982: Film star Paul Newman teams up with his good friend A.E. Hotchner to make available to the public their annual Christmas present to their friends. The pair has been mixing up salad dressing for years, combining oil, vinegar, and spices and presenting them in old wine bottles. The dressing launches Newman's Own all-natural food line. During the rest of the decade, the pair is busy. They introduce Marinara Sauce and Mushroom Sauce (1983), Popcorn in Jars (1984), Butter and Natural Microwave Popcorn (1986), Sockarooni Sauce (1986), and Lemonade (1987).

1982: Wolfgang Puck, 31, opens Spago restaurant in Los Angeles. He popularizes gourmet pizza and by 1990 is grossing $6 million a year.

1982: General Electric offers the first 24-hours-a-day, 7-days-a-week consumer information service.

1982: General Mills opens the first Olive Garden restaurant.

1982: Mrs. Butterworth's Pancake Mix is introduced.

1982: Jenny Craig, Inc., a weight-loss program, is founded by San Diego entrepreneur Sid Craig and his wife, Jenny.

1983: Stephan Pyles opens Routh Street Cafe in Dallas.

1984: Chef Paul Prudhomme blackens his first fish.

1984: Nearly 20 cents of the food dollar is spent on "light" and diet foods. This doesn't include money spent on cottage cheese, fruits, vegetables, and skim milk.

1984: McCormick introduces Reduced Sodium Garlic and Onion Salt. Also new are Lemon and Pepper Seasoning, Season-All, and Fried Chicken Seasoning.

1985: Coca-Cola announces that it is replacing its formula with a sweeter Coke designed for younger tastes. It is a fiasco—leading to a reintroduction of "old" Coke under the name Classic. The whole affair takes on the dimension of Ford's Edsel.

1985: Boston Chicken has its beginnings in a Newton, Mass., fast-food restaurant.

1986: Swanson replaces the tray in its TV dinner with a plastic model that can be microwaved.

1986: Advanced Fresh Concepts opens in Compton, Calif. The company trains sushi chefs and outfits space within grocery stores to sell fresh-made sushi in ready-to-serve packages. By the end of the century, AFC has 500 sushi counters in 42 states and Canada.

Frito-Lay

1986: Chester Cheetah becomes the spokesperson for Cheetos: "It's Not Easy Being Cheesy."

Kraft

1986: Olympic marathon runner Brian Maxwell and his wife, Jennifer, develop a high-energy bar for athletes in their Berkeley, Calif., kitchen. Introduced as the PowerBar, the snacks are hits with athletes as well as with the exercising public. By the end of the 1990s, the company is a line aimed at the breakfast market. It also has PowerBar ProteinPlus, which contains 25 grams of protein, and Power-Bar GelPlus, a high-carbohydrate jellied mixture consumers squeeze from a pouch into their mouths for an instant jolt of energy.

1986: McDonald's and Burger King stop frying their food in beef tallow and start releasing nutritional and ingredients information about their food.

1987: Gene splicing allows the patenting of new life forms.

1987: EdgeCraft Corp,. introduces the Chef's Choice Diamond Home Sharpener and employs Craig Claiborne as spokesman.

1987: Microwave oven sales reach a record 12.6 million. Kenmore is the largest-selling brand.

1987: Snapple introduces bottled iced tea, creating a new soft-drink category.

1988: There has been enough innovation in the fresh processed fruit and vegetable sector that the National Association of Fresh Produce Processors is organized. By the end of the century, supermarkets are stocked with already washed and cut cabbage, broccoli, cauliflower, salads and coleslaws, carrots, onions, stir-fry vegetables, fruit salads, grapes, melons, and onions.

1988: Boboli pizza crusts—ready-made baked crusts—are introduced.

1988: Oscar Mayer Lunchables are introduced.

1988: American manufacturers introduce 972 new microwaveable products.

1989: Spurred by a *60 Minutes* report, parents run scared from apples because of reports linking alar, a ripening agent, with cancer.

AFC

1989: Tapping into the low-fat mindset of the country, Frito-Lay formulates the entire Rold Gold pretzel line, a brand they have owned since 1961. (The first commercial pretzel bakery opened in the United States in Litiz, Penn., in 1861.)

1989: Fresh Express in Salinas, Calif., bags "packaged" salads. The bag is designed to regulate oxygen to keep washed, cut lettuce fresh for up to two weeks with no preservatives. The first salad is iceberg, by far America's favorite lettuce. But by the end of the century, mixes include radicchio, mesclun, and frisee. Some also include, packaged in separate bags, dressing and croutons. By 2000, packaged salad sales top $1 billion.

1989: Reynolds rolls out its Plastic Wrap in colors, geared to wrapping holiday treats. The move ignites growth in a stagnant category.

Fresh Express

1989: ConAgra CEO Charles Harper introduces the Healthy Choice line of frozen low-fat, low-cholesterol, low-sodium foods his company developed after he had a heart attack.

1990–1999

After the roaring 1980s, Americans turned to healthy food, "alternative" beverages, and lots of takeout fare. Hung over from the excesses of the 1980s, America sobered up in the 1990s.

The stock market crash of 1987 had put the skids on opulent new restaurant openings. Alar-on-apples worries and salmonella outbreaks had consumers concerned about the food supply.

Warnings from the American Heart Association and the American Medical Association had people comparing cholesterol rates and fiber intake. The Food and Drug Administration issued new dietary guidelines, placing an emphasis on grains and vegetables and limiting meats and fats.

Taking note of America's fixation with weight and health, food manufacturers responded with products like Nabisco's SnackWell's cookies and Lay's baked chips. We ate them up, but we still got fatter.

Huge technological advances made our lives easier (fax machines, cellular phones, pagers, and the Internet), but Americans were spending 50 cents of every food dollar on prepared foods, citing time as the reason not to cook.

Despite these concerns with health and time, the goddess-of-things-gracious, Martha Stewart, became the symbol of food and living for many. For so many, in fact, that she was able to take her company public in 1999, making a fortune telling time-

ABOVE: AMERICANS COOK LESS AT THE END OF THE CENTURY, BUT THE KITCHEN TOYS GET MORE GLITZ.
Subzero

RIGHT: TOLL HOUSE COOKIES TOO DIFFICULT TO MAKE? NESTLE MAKES THEM FOR US (AND ESPECIALLY FOR THE CHILDREN IN THE HOUSE) BY MIXING THE DOUGH, SCORING IT ON A TRAY AND SELLING IT FROM THE GROCER'S REFRIGERATOR CASE. IT'S ALL IN THE NAME OF EASE FOR THE CONSUMER.
Nestle

172

strapped consumers how to spin sugar, roof their gingerbread houses with gold leaf, and carve ice sculptures with chain saws. Consumers gobbled up Stewart's television shows and her cookbooks and her magazines and her Kmart-brand sheets. But they also gobbled up home-meal replacements, the ready-to-reheat fresh-made meals provided by food-to-go specialist EatZi's and, by the end of the decade, almost all grocery stores. Stewart may be good theater (as was the popular Food TV Network), but more and more America wanted someone else to do the cooking.

As the economy picked up in the middle of the decade, the restaurant scene boomed. But instead of the excessive consumption of the 1980s, the money driving the new surge in dining out was coming from families pushed for time. Even fast-food restaurants began offering once-exotic items like Caesar salad. Southwestern fare refused to fade (as the Cajun rage had), and dishes such as tortilla soup were served by mainstream restaurants. And—in the typical extremes of all things American—steakhouses boomed in a nation obsessed with health. The style du jour was "fusion," ingredients from various cuisines combined to make a new whole.

LEFT: TIME IS NO LONGER NEEDED TO ENJOY BREWED ICE TEA. Lipton

ABOVE: WITH A STARBUCKS COFFEE SHOP ON ALMOST EVERY CORNER IN AMERICA, FOOD PRODUCERS RUSH TO GRAB SOME OF THE MARKET. KRAFT INTRODUCES CAPPUCCINO COOLERS IN 1998. Kraft

BELOW: THE FOOD COMPANIES KNOW THEIR COMPETITION IS NO LONGER JUST ONE ANOTHER. WITH 50 PERCENT OF THE FOOD DOLLAR GOING FOR ITEMS PREPARED OUTSIDE THE HOME, AND HALF OF THAT GOING TO FAST-FOOD OPERATIONS, ITEMS SUCH AS SCRAMBLES, A FROZEN PORTABLE BREAKFAST, JOIN THE FROZEN FOOD CASE. Pillsbury

But it wasn't just complete meals Americans ordered out. They realized they could get drinks to go: portable meals pumped up with protein and vitamins they could drink in their cars.

Jamba Juice opened shops in California in 1990, and by the end of the decade it was the leader in the juice-bar category. In fact, the 1990s could be labeled the "alternative-beverage decade," with an explosion of smoothies, sports drinks, flavored waters, designer sodas, and flavored bottled teas.

As the century turned into the millennium, the influence of ancient cultures and our own hippie past pushed an ever-increasing addition of herbs like ginseng and Saint-John's-wort into everything from snack chips to distilled water. And mainstream manufacturers also put "value-added" ingredients in products, like calcium in dried pasta and salad dressing juiced up with vitamin E.

We haven't yet substituted a pill for dinner, as was once predicted. However, the line between the drugstore and the kitchen is quickly fading.

America wants dinner fast, they want it to taste good, and they want it to have as little fat as possible.

QUICK FAJITAS
WITH PICO DE GALLO

[SERVES 4]

MARINADE

1 pound round or top sirloin steak

2 tablespoons fresh lime juice

2 teaspoon vegetable oil

2 large cloves garlic, crushed

PICO DE GALLO

1 cup tomato, seeded and chopped

½ cup zucchini, diced

¼ cup fresh cilantro, chopped

¼ cup prepared salsa

1 tablespoon fresh lime juice

FOR SERVING

8 small flour tortillas, warmed

Sour cream

Guacamole

Chopped green onions

PLACE BEEF steak in plastic bag; add marinade ingredients, turning to coat. Close bag securely and marinate in refrigerator 20 to 30 minutes, turning once.

Meanwhile in medium bowl, combine Pico de Gallo ingredients; mix well.

Remove steak from marinade; discard marinade. Place steak on rack in broiler pan so surface of meat is 2 to 3 inches from heat. Broil 12 to 13 minutes (9 to 12 minutes for top sirloin steak) for medium rare doneness, turning occasionally.

Trim fat from steak; carve crosswise into very thin slices. Serve beef in tortillas with sour cream, guacamole, chopped green onions, and Pico de Gallo.

—www.beeftips.com

Chiquita

CHIQUITA PUTS A FACE ON
PRODUCE WITH ITS MISS
CHIQUITA BRANDING.
Chiquita

OUT OF THIS WORLD
for QUALITY
and FLAVOR

CHIQUITA BANDED BANANAS

Junior & Dot Together At Last!

Two Concession Classics - *Junior Mints*® and *Mason Dots*® - are appearing together at theatres around the country. Dots' super assortment of five fruit flavors and Junior Mints' creamy combination of cool mint and dark milk chocolate have been the choice of movie goer's for years. Make sure your concession features the double selling power of these two favorites - *Junior and Dot together at last!*

Contact your local Tootsie Roll Distributor Representative for complete order information.

© Copyright, 1994

Tootsie Roll Industries, Inc.
7401 S. Cicero Avenue • Chicago, IL 60629

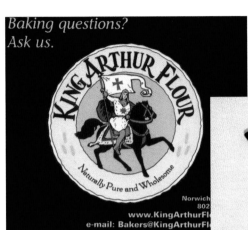

Baking questions?
Ask us.

KING ARTHUR FLOUR
Naturally Pure and Wholesome

Norwich
802
www.KingArthurFl
e-mail: Bakers@KingArthurFl

HomeGrocer.com™

all Customer Service at 1-800-688-0201 or e-mail service@HomeGrocer.com

KRAFT · Interactive Kitchen

good food for busy lives

Come visit us at
http://www.kraftfoods.com

NABISCO WORLD .COM

3 GRAMS of FAT OR LE

Häagen-Dazs
LOW FAT
VANILLA
ICE CREAM

ABOVE: FOOD PRODUCERS GO CYBER AND PROMOTE THEIR PRODUCTS AND RECIPES ON THE INTERNET. SEVERAL COMPANIES TRY TO FACILITATE INTERNET GROCERY ORDERING AND DELIVERY, BUT THE LOGISTICS ARE AWKWARD AND FEW INROADS ARE MADE.

ABOVE: WE WANT OUR ICE CREAM AND WE WANT TO EAT IT, TOO. EVEN PREMIUM INDULGENCES TRY TO OFFER A LOWER-FAT ALTERNATIVE. Pillsbury

CHICKEN FILLETS
IN TOMATO-WINE SAUCE

[SERVES 4]

1 pound chicken breast fillets cut into 8 pieces

½ teaspoon coarsely ground pepper

½ teaspoon salt

1 can (16 ounces) whole tomatoes, quartered, liquid retained

2 purple onions, sliced

2 cloves garlic, minced

1 teaspoon basil

½ cup white wine

SPRAY NON-STICK fry pan with butter-flavored non-stick vegetable spray. Heat to medium high, add chicken, and brown about 2 minutes on each side. Remove chicken to warm platter and sprinkle with pepper and salt.

Drain all liquid from tomatoes (should be about 1 cup); pour tomato liquid into fry pan and add onion, garlic, and basil. Bring to a boil, reduce heat, cover and simmer until onion is tender, about 5 minutes. Add tomatoes, wine, and chicken; cover and simmer about 15 minutes. Remove cover and cook on medium temperature about 5 minutes. Serve on fettuccini noodles.

—www.eatchicken.com

ABOVE: RECENTLY DEFEATED GOVERNORS ANN RICHARDS AND MARIO CUOMO ADMIT THAT THINGS MUST CHANGE, EVEN THE FLAVORS OF DORITOS IN THIS TV SPOT. Frito-Lay

NEWMAN'S OWN
SALSA

So good it oughta be outlawed!

EGGNOG CREME BRULEE

[SERVES 8]

3 cups heavy cream

5 egg yolks

2 eggs

½ cup white sugar

2 tablespoons dark rum

1 tablespoon brandy

1 teaspoon vanilla

½ teaspoon nutmeg

Hot water

½ cup firmly packed brown sugar, divided

HEAT OVEN to 325 degrees. Place eight 6-ounce ramekins or custard cups in 15-by-10-by-1 inch baking pan.

Heat cream in medium saucepan just to a simmer. Remove from heat.

In medium bowl, combine egg yolks and eggs; beat well. Stir in white sugar until combined. With wire whisk, stir in hot cream until well-blended. Stir in rum, brandy, vanilla, and nutmeg. Pour mixture into ramekins.

Place pan in oven; pour hot water into pan until it's ½- to ¾-inch up sides of ramekins.

Bake for 30 to 35 minutes or until centers are just set. Carefully remove from oven. Place cups on wire rack to cool. Cool 30 minutes. Refrigerate at least 3 hours or overnight.

Before serving, place ramekins in the 15-by-10-by-1-inch baking pan. Top each with 1 tablespoon brown sugar. Broil 4 to 6 minutes from heat for 1 to 2 minutes or until sugar is melted. (Watch closely.) Store in refrigerator.

— Pillsbury

CENTRAL MARKET:
GROCERIES OF THE FUTURE

B Y THE 1990S, grocery stores are casting wide with their nets, stocking school supplies and potting soil and batteries. They lease space to banks and film processors, hoping to snag shoppers as a one-stop service.

But one operation, viewed by industry watchers as the harbinger of 21st century food retailing, goes an entirely different direction.

Central Market sells nothing but food—75,000-square-feet of food. And while it's a global mix that consumers know, no where else in the world is it seen in one such huge, organized package.

The cheese counter carries 700 varieties from Cornish yarg to French Saint Andre. The 100-foot seafood counter stocks some of its wares, live, in tanks kept at three temperature zones—Atlantic, Pacific and Gulf of Mexico. The meat department has recipes for 60 varieties of sausage and makes 25 of them daily.

The wine department stocks 2,000 labels, the beer section 400. In the fall, the produce section stocks 25 varieties of apples and four colors of pumpkins.

But in the midst of all this food, there is not to be found a Coca Cola, a Budweiser, or cat litter. And despite the lessons of the past 100 years about the power of American mass merchandising, the customers eat it up.

By the end of the century, the original Austin store was drawing 500,000 visitors a year, second only to the State Capitol as Austin's top tourist attraction.

Food, despite a century of billboards, golden arches and TV bombardment, still hits consumers at a viseral, sensory level.

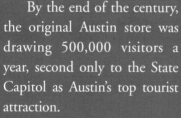

BARBARA BUSH'S BATCH

[Yields 3 dozen]

1 cup plus 2 tablespoons sifted all-purpose flour

½ teaspoon baking soda

½ teaspoon salt

½ cup butter, softened

⅓ cup firmly packed brown sugar

⅓ cup white sugar

1 egg

1½ teaspoons very hot water

½ teaspoon vanilla extract

1 cup semisweet chocolate chips

Preheat oven to 375 degrees. Sift together flour, baking soda, and salt onto wax paper. Beat butter, brown sugar, white sugar, and egg in large bowl with electric mixer until fluffy, about 3 minutes.

Beat in hot water and vanilla. Gradually beat in flour mixture until blended and smooth. Stir in chocolate chips.

Drop dough by well-rounded measuring teaspoonfuls onto large greased baking sheet. Bake for 10 minutes or until golden. Cool on sheet on wire rack 1 minute. Remove cookies from sheet onto wire rack to cool completely.

— *Family Circle* magazine

ABOVE: Maxwell House Lite, a reduced-caffeine coffee, in introduced nationally. Kraft

HILLARY CLINTON'S CHIPS

[YIELDS 7½ DOZEN]

1½ cups unsifted all-purpose flour

1 teaspoon salt

1 teaspoon baking soda

1 cup solid vegetable shortening

1 cup firmly packed light brown sugar

½ cup granulated sugar

1 teaspoon vanilla

2 eggs

2 cups old-fashioned rolled oats

1 package (12 ounces) semisweet chocolate chips

Preheat oven to 350 degrees. Grease baking sheets. Combine flour, salt, and baking soda on wax paper. Beat together shortening, sugars, and vanilla in large bowl with electric mixer until creamy. Add eggs, beating until light and fluffy. Gradually beat in flour mixture and rolled oats. Stir in chocolate chips.

Drop batter by well-rounded measuring teaspoonfuls onto baking sheets. Bake for 8 to 10 minutes or until golden. Cool cookies on sheets on wire rack 2 minutes. Remove cookies from sheet onto wire rack to cool completely.

— *Family Circle* magazine

ABOVE: Low-fat doesn't cut it anymore. The demanding consumer wants it tasty and fat free. Kraft

BETTY CROCKER'S ABOUT FACE

Betty crocker, the longtime symbol of baking for Americans, turns 75. To celebrate, General Mills remakes the image of their corporate representative from a computerized composite of 75 women.

Betty Crocker is first rendered by artist Neysa McMein in 1936. That likeness of Betty is a composite of several women in the company's Home Service Department.

In 1955 Betty gets her first makeover. After a vote by 1,600 women across the nation, illustrator Hilda Taylor's younger, less stern rendering of Betty becomes the symbol.

In the 1960s, Betty gets two lifts from artist Joe Bowler. All the gray is now gone from her hair and she looks 20 years younger.

Betty becomes businesslike in 1972 in her depiction by Jerome Ryan. Women are off to the office, and Betty is no exception.

By 1980 Betty becomes comfortable with her dual role of work and home, and the softness of her hair and the more casual neckline of her blouse says as much. In 1986 Harriet Perchik depicted Betty as younger, but comfortable and competent.

The 1996 image of Betty is still without gray in her hair, but the diversity of America's population is evident. Betty's skin is no longer Nordic and her eyes are no longer blue.

ABOVE: Betty Crocker's looks change over the years, and unlike a real person, she gets younger. General Mills

Introducing something that needs no introduction.

The great taste and texture of *Kellogg's* *Rice Krispies Treats*™ squares need no introduction.

For over 50 years, our simple recipe has been a favorite with everyone. Now it'll be a big hit with you too, because our new foil-wrapped *Rice Krispies Treats*™ squares mean you can give your customers the great homemade taste they know and love.

Isn't that the best news since your mom introduced you to the *Kellogg's* *Rice Krispies Treats*™ recipe?

Kellogg's
FOODSERVICE
1-800-554-1971

LEFT AND ABOVE: CONSUMERS HAVE BECOME SUCH NON-COOKS THAT SMART MANUFACTURERS, WHO ONCE PAID LOTS OF MONEY TO DEVELOP RECIPES FOR CUSTOMERS TO MAKE WITH THEIR PRODUCTS NOW MAKE THOSE PRODUCTS FOR THE CUSTOMER AS WELL. RICE KRISPIES TREATS, A CHILD PARTY FAVORITE THAT CALLS FOR THREE INGREDIENTS, IS MADE BY KELLOGG'S AND PACKAGED IN INDIVIUDAL SERVINGS—PERFECT FOR LUNCH BOXES. Kellogg's

RIGHT: IN THE 1990S LIFE REACHES WARP SPEED. PARENTS NO LONGER NEED TO TAKE THE TIME TO BREW ICED TEA OR STIR CHOCOLATE POWDER INTO MILK. AND BETTER YET, THESE DRINKS ARE PACKAGED SO THE FAMILY CAN DRINK AND DRIVE. Nestle and Lipton

Oxo

1990: OXO Good Grips premieres. The line earns the Tylenol/Arthritis Foundation award for its wide, easy-to-hold design. The peeler is the best-selling item in the line.

1990: The U.S. Department of Agriculture introduces the Food Guide Pyramid.

1990: "I do not like broccoli. And I haven't liked it since I was a little boy and my mother made me eat it. And I'm President of the United States, and I'm not going to eat any more broccoli."

—George Bush

1990: The first fully recyclable plastic ketchup bottle hits supermarket shelves.

1990: Consumer plastic bag recycling begins with a supermarket collection site networks.

1991: Almost 66 percent of married women are working or looking for work, compared with 46 percent in 1973.

1991: McDonalds introduces the McLean Deluxe, a lower-fat burger that is eventually shelved because of consumer lack of interest.

1991: Crisco Sticks are introduced.

1991: U.S. sales of salsa pass those of ketchup by $40 million.

1991: Only 51 percent of Americans older than 10 drink coffee, down from 75 percent in 1971.

1991: The night before the U.S. bombing of Baghdad, Domino's delivers 101 pizzas to the Pentagon instead of the usual three.

1992: Hillary Rodham Clinton and Barbara Bush duke it out with rival cookie recipes published in *Family Circle*.

1992: Almost half of U.S. supermarkets have recycling available for plastic bags.

1992: AriZona and Nestea bottled iced teas are introduced.

1992: Charlie's Lunch Kit is introduced as the first mix-it-yourself portable tuna meal.

1992: Nestle acquires Perrier bottled water, which includes the Arrowhead, Calistoga, Oasis, Deer Park, Poland Springs, and Zephyrhills brands.

Proctor and Gamble

1992: Almost 50 percent of all Tupperware consultants have full-time jobs in addition to selling the plastic products. And their clients are changing, too. No longer are the consultants simply selling; often they're teaching how to cook, as well. Food preparation and microwave cooking become a part of the Tupperware message. Parties are no longer relegated to the home—some are held in the workplace during lunch hours. And Tupper-ware goes international, offering products like the Kimchi Keeper and the Japanese Bento Box.

1992: Bio Foods is founded by entrepreneurs who've obtained the rights to a moderate-carbohydrate, moderate-protein nutrition bar. Originally intended for people with special dietary needs (diabetics, heart patients), the company sees a broader market. Balance Bars become available in gyms, convenience stores, and grocery stores and catch on with a public that is exercising and watching its nutritional intake.

1992: Basketball greats Kareem Abdul-Jabbar and Larry Bird advertise for Lay's Potato Chips' new formulation. The motto becomes "Too Good to Eat Just One."

1993: U.S. annual per-capita egg consumption falls to 232, down from 321 in 1960, as the country becomes consumed with worries about cholesterol.

1993: Jason Alexander, one of the stars of the popular *Seinfeld* TV comedy, becomes the everyman image for Rold Gold pretzels.

1993: Boca Burger, a soy-based protein burger, is introduced by Max Shondor, a Florida-based natural food restauranteur. By the end of the decade, the line expands from the flavors of the Original Boca Burger to breakfast patties, meatless tenders, and meatless nuggets.

1993: The nation's first 24-hour food channel, The Food Network, goes on the air.

1993: Tootsie Roll acquires the caramel and chocolate brands of Warner-Lambert Co., which includes Junior Mints, Sugar Daddy, Sugar Babies, and Charleston Chews.

1993: SnackWell cookies and crackers, a low-fat line, is introduced.

1994: Campbell Soup Co. buys Pace Foods of San Antonio, the world's largest producer of salsas and other Mexican sauces.

1994: Miss Chiquita turns 50, looking sexier than ever. Created in 1944 by artist Dik Browne (creator of the Campbell Soup Kids and "Hagar the Horrible"), Miss Chiquita begins life as an animated banana. In the late 1980s, Oscar Grillo (creator of the Pink Panther) turns her into a woman. By the end of the millennium, Miss Chiquita is full-fledged hot stuff and bananas are the no. 1 fruit consumed in America.

1994: Denny's agrees to pay more than $54 million to settle lawsuits filed by thousands of black customers alleging discrimination.

1994: Fruitopia bottled fruit beverages are introduced.

1994: Hungry Jack Syrup is marketed in a microwaveable plastic bottle.

1995: Recently defeated Governors Ann Richards (Texas) and Mario Cuomo (New York) discuss the need to embrace change in a "Doritos: Flavors The Way You Look at Life" TV commercial. The ad airs during the Super Bowl telecast, a venue known for innovative, highly-anticipated advertising.

Kraft

1995: Blue Bell introduces the nation's first full line of bite-size mini-frozen snacks, from fruit ices to chocolate-dipped cones.

1995: DiGiorno Rising Crust Pizza is introduced.

1996: Although introduced in the United States in 1987, electric bread makers reach a point of affordability in the 1990s, and more than 15 million are sold.

1996: The Grocery Manufacturers of America announces that grocery packaging discards (the portion of packaging that the consumer throws away) dropped more than 14 percent from 1980 to 1993.

1996: The Food and Drug Administration approves Olestra, the first fat substitute.

1996: Lay's Baked Potato Crisps are introduced.

1996: Dunkin' Donuts introduces freshly baked bagels. By 1997 the company is the country's largest retailer of bagels.

1996: Four of five grocery bags used are plastic.

1997: *The Joy of Cooking* is overhauled and reissued.

1997: V8 Splash is introduced.

1997: Consumers spend $10.3 billion for food home delivery and mail order. This is a 5.6 percent increase from 1996. About 50 percent of the food dollar is spent on food prepared outside the home.

1997: Irradiation of meat is approved by the Food and Drug Administration. Spices have long been irradiated, but a general mistrust of all things nuclear and protests by well-organized chefs and natural-food producers leave the nation's consumers confused. Meat companies wait to jump on the irradiation bandwagon, leery of what marketplace reaction will be.

1997: Newman's Own continues its winning ways, introducing almost 20 products during the 1990s, including six varieties of salsa, Parisienne Dijon Lime Dressing, Steak Sauce, and Say Cheese sauce. By 1999 Newman will have donated more than $100 million to charities in the U.S. and foreign countries where the products are sold.

1998: Potato sprouts carried aloft on the space shuttle *Columbia* produce the first food grown in outer space.

1998: Frozen Skillet Sensations, a fryable entree combination, is introduced as an even-quicker way to get dinner on the table. Green Giant has been offering Creat A Meal in the same category since 1993.

1998: Fat-free Pringles, using Olean, are introduced. Frito-Lay introduces the Wow! line of chips using the same product.

1998: Organic farmers, marketers, chefs, and consumers send more than 280,000 protest letters, prompting the U.S. Department of Agriculture secretary to withdraw a proposal to allow food to be labeled organic even if it is irradiated to kill germs, genetically engineered, or subjected to sewage sludge or chemical spraying. The USDA continues to work on guidelines to have a national standard for organic food.

1999: To celebrate its 130th anniversary, Heinz offers its ketchup in the classic eight-paneled glass bottle with the Keystone label.

1999: Pillsbury rolls out the OneStep Brownie, already prepared dough in a pan ready for baking. The company introduced One Step Cookies two years earlier. Nestle enters the game about the same time with Refrigerateed Chocolate Chip Cookie Bars and Brownie Bars, prepared doughs that are scored into portion sizes ready for baking.

1999: About 59 percent of all women work outside the home, averaging 72 cents for every dollar earned by men.

1999: Genetically engineered corn is found to contribute to the death rate of monarch butterflies.

Heinz

1999: The Food and Drug Administration allows manufacturers of whole-grain cereals and breads to advertise that those foods help fight heart disease and cancer.

1999: Prepackaged convenience foods are the fastest-growing segment of the natural-foods market, which is seeing a 20 percent annual growth rate. Consumers are gobbling up soy-based frankfurters, veggie burgers, frozen tofu desserts, and vegetable burritos.

1999: What Fannie Farmer was to the beginning of the century and Julia Child was to the after-war years, Martha Stewart is to the end of the century.

A multitasker of the first order, Stewart moves from modeling in college to selling stocks after she graduates. But renovating a historic Connecticut farmhouse changes her life and those of legions of American women who become devoted fans.

Beginning as a caterer, Stewart realizes that this newest generation of women is intimidated by entertaining, cowed by the kitchen, and hopeless as decorators.

Farmer showed middle-class women they could indeed cook by being regimented and having order in their kitchen. Child showed them that it could be fun—that there is a cosmos of food out there to explore. But Martha Stewart shows them how to do it with style.

Stewart writes books, produces television shows, designs a line of housewares and garden goods for K-Mart, and sells other products she designs via mail and the Internet.

And finally, like all good ideas in the high-flying 1990s, she becomes a corporation and goes public on the New York Stock Exchange. In typical I-can-do-it-all style, on the day of her Initial Public Offering, she passes out muffins to brokers entering the exchange.

1999: The average household works 40 days to buy its food for the year and spends 11 percent of household income on the annual food bill.

1999: General Electric introduces its Advantium Oven. The appliance uses Speedcook technology to cook food 4 to 14 times faster than a conventional oven cooks.

Index

SOURCES

A WORK LIKE this is impossible without the good records, determination and skullduggery of souls more tenacious than me.

Because this is very much a social history, the sources used were varied, and in some cases, unusual. However, food is folklore that quickly becomes history, so getting the facts down before they disappear into the ether (or gelatin mold) of tomorrow is vital.

There are a couple of people who I'd like to thank on a personal, as well as a professional level, for going above and beyond professional courtesies.

John Mariani was a gent when I first wrote the newspaper series, shipping me a huge bundle of original art he had used in his books. All he asked in return was that I assuage the hunger of his son and his college roommates with a few pounds of ribs and some barbecue brisket. Federal Express never smelled so good.

At Kraft, Jill Saletta and her staff went through rows of records and years of details to find dates and images of their company's huge impact on the country's eating habits. And at Nestle, Davina Geuenstein and Yasmeen Muqtasid did the same.

A special thank you to all the public relations people in faceless corporations across America who function as their employer's husband—never forgetting an anniversary or a birthday, always alerting the media when a product turns 50—or 150.

And to anyone I've inadvertently omitted from following list, the oversight is purely my own.

Anderson, Jean. *American Century Cookbook.* New York, New York: Clarkson Potter, 1997.

Brenner, Joel Glenn. *The Emperors of Chocolate: Inside the Secret World of Hershey and Mars.* New york, New York: Random House, 1999.

Chariton, Wallace O. *Neighbor, How Long Has it Been? The Story of Wolf Brand Chili.* Plano, Texas: Five Points Press, 1998.

Clarke, Alison J. *Tupperware: The Promise of Plastic in 1950s America.* Washinton, D.C: Smithsonian Institution Press, 1999.

Collins, Douglas. *America's Favorite Food: The Story of Campbell Soup.* New York, New York: Henry N. Abrams,1994.

Dr Pepper King of Beverages: Centennial Edition. Dallas, Texas: Published by Dr Pepper Co, 1986.

Fussell, Betty. *The Story of Corn.* New York, New York: Random House, 1992.

Gardner, David and Tom. *The Motley Fool's Rule Breakers, Rule Makers: The Foolish guide to Picking Stocks.* New York, New York: Simon & Schuster, 1999.

Ierley, Merritt. *The Comforts of Home: The American House and the Evolution of Modern Convenience.* New york, New York: Crown, 1999.

Ierley, Merritt. *Open House: A Guided Tour of the American Home, 1637–Present.* New York, New York: Henry Holt, 1999.

Jones, Evans. *American Food: The Gastronomic Story.* Woodstock, New York: Crescent Books, 1990.

Kasuba, Victoria and Kohn, Karen. *America at Home: A Celebration of American Housewares.* Rosemount, Illinois: National Housewares Manufacturers Association, 1997.

Levenstein, Harvey. *Revolution at the Table: The Transformation of the American Diet.* New York, New York: Oxford, 1988.

Liles, Allen. *Oh Thank Heaven: The Story of the Southland Corporation.* Dallas, Texas: Published by Southland, 1976.

Lovegren, Sylvia. *Fashionable Food.* New York, New York: Macmillan, 1995.

Lupton, Ellen. *Mechanical Brides. Woman and Machines from Home to Office.* New York, New York: Cooper-Hewitt National Museum of Design & Princeton Architectural Press, 1993.

Mariani, John. *America Eats Out: An Illustrated History of Restaurants, Taverns, Coffee Shops, Speakeasies, and Other Establishments That Have Fed Us for 350 Years.* New York, New York: Williams Morrow, 1991.

Mariani, John. *The Dictionary of American Food and Drink.* New York, New York: Hearst, 1994.

Nathan, Joan. *Jewish Cooking in America.* New York, New York: Knopf, 1998.

Plante, Ellen M. *The American Kitchen: 1700 to the Present From Hearth to Highrise.* New York, New York: Facts on File, 1993.

Ridenour, Alan. *Offbeat Food: Adventures in an Omnivorous World.* Santa Monica, California: Santa Monica Press, 2000.

Rochem, Richard De and Root, Waverley. *Eating in America: A History.* New York, New York: William Morrow, 1976.

Rukeyser, Louis. *The Book of Lists.* New York, New York: Owl/Henry Holt, 1997.

Sack, Daniel. *Whitebread Protestants: Food and Religion in American Culture.* New York, New York: St. Martin's Press, 2000.

Shapiro, Laura. *Perfection Salad: Women and Cooking at the Turn of the Century.* New York, New York: North Point Press, 1986.

Sokolov, Raymond A. *Fading Feast: A Compendium of Disappearing American Regional Foods.* New York, New York: Farrar Straus & Giroux, 1983.

Stevenson, Katherine Cole. *Houses by Mail: A Guide to Houses from Sears, Roebuck and Company.* Washington, D.C: Preservation Press, 1986.

Trager, James. *The Food Chronology: A Food Lover's Compendium of Events and Anecdotes from Prehistory to the Present.* New York, New York: Owl Books, 1995.

Witzel, Michael Karl and Young-Witzel, Gyvel. *Soda Pop! From Miracle Medicine to Pop Culture.* Stillwater, Minnesota: Voyageur Press, 1998.

100 of the Best Recipes for 100 Years from McCormick. Hunt Valley, Maryland: Published by McCormick, 1989.